ORIENTAL RUGS

I Caucasian. Shirvan. 4 ft. × 7 ft. The field is decorated with a diaper of flowering plant forms; the innermost guard-stripe, which is white, sets this off in relief. The middle band of the border has a Herati pattern based on mock Kufic letters (as in many 16th century Anatolian carpets) in place of the more usual serrated leaves. This border is paler at the bottom of the carpet than on the other three sides. The twin guard-stripes have a design of carnations.

ORIENTAL RUGS

an illustrated guide

by

HERMANN HAACK

edited and translated by

GEORGE AND CORNELIA
WINGFIELD DIGBY

FABER AND FABER LIMITED

24 Russell Square

London

Published in Germany under the title of
ECHTE TEPPICHE
By F. Bruckmann K. G. Munich

First published in England mcmlx
by Faber and Faber Limited
24 Russell Square London W.C.1
Third Impression mcmlxiv
Fourth Impression mcmlxvii
Printed in Great Britain by
R. MacLehose and Company Limited
The University Press Glasgow

CONTENTS

7

ILLUSTRATIONS

COLOUR PLATES

MONOCHROME PLATES

Illustrations

FOREWORD

This book has been designed as a guide for the layman who has no special knowledge, but who wishes to acquire an understanding of oriental rugs and carpets. With its wide range of illustrations it will acquaint him with the better-known carpet types and their classification, which is explained in the text together with the considerations, technical and otherwise, which condition the making of hand-knotted rugs. It is hoped that it will enable him to cultivate a taste of his own, based on the elements of a sound knowledge of carpet making in Persia and other lands of the Near East and lead him to distinguish good rugs from indifferent ones, or actual copies. It is also hoped that this book will be useful to those who buy rugs for the furnishing of their homes as well as those with the collector's instinct, since many classes of good oriental rugs are by no means unduly expensive, even though the rarest and finest carpets may be beyond the reach of all save the very wealthy.

Most of the rugs illustrated in this book are taken from the collections of Messrs. L. Bernheimer of Munich and have not hitherto been reproduced. The author and publishers have to thank Consul Otto Bernheimer, an acknowledged authority in this field, for his help and advice in selecting the carpets and rugs for illustration.

In making the English translation, the text has been freely edited and somewhat reduced, so that this new corpus of oriental rugs and carpets of all types can be presented to the English reading public as an illustrated guide. The historical section and the note on conservation have been rewritten. In the text the words 'carpets' and 'rugs' are almost synonymous, but whilst the larger or showier floor coverings are specifically termed carpets, the word rug is applied particularly to the smaller and less pretentious pieces.

I

HISTORICAL NOTE

It is only since the beginning of the sixteenth century that oriental carpets have been preserved in any numbers. Their early history remains obscure and the many theories put forward about their origins in place and time are largely hypothetical. Since the beginning of the sixteenth century, however, the evidence is not only backed by the considerable number of carpets which have survived, but also by representations of them in paintings by the Italian and Flemish masters, as well as in oriental illuminated manuscripts. From this evidence it is clear that there was more than one school of design and weaving at that time. First there was the Persian school of carpet weaving, which was to reach its zenith in the sixteenth century under the Shahs of the Safavid dynasty. This great period of carpet weaving in Persia worked under the lively and brilliant influence of the court painters and illuminators; it continued until at least the generation after the death of Shah Abbas I (1507–1628). Secondly there was the school of carpet weaving centred in Turkish Anatolia which favoured geometrical patterns and relied on polygons, star-forms and arabesque scrolls, in contrast to the more naturalistic Persian patterns. This style, with some modifications, was also current in Armenia and the Caucasus. Thirdly, there was an important manufacture of carpets in Cairo which reflected the Mamluk style of that period. Finally, it should not be forgotten that Moorish Spain was a great producer of carpets and some of the best fifteenth century carpets which have survived originated

13

in that country. Their style largely reflects that of Turkish Anatolia, but unlike them, they were usually woven with the single warp knot.

The difficulty of reconstructing the history of carpet weaving before the latter part of the fifteenth century is increased by the fact that the literary references to carpets are very uncertain, since it is difficult to distinguish the difference between words used to denote floor and divan covers, coverlets of finer texture, and wall hangings. It is nearly always uncertain from the Greek or Latin text whether a true pile carpet is being referred to or not. Moreover, the distinction between pile carpets and floor or divan covers of a lighter texture was not so marked in oriental countries as, from a western point of view, one might suppose. Furniture was far less used in the rooms, and it was customary to discard footwear at the door of the house on entering, and to sit or recline on the floor directly upon carpeting.

In the lands where carpets were made, therefore, there was a much closer human relationship with the carpet on the floor or the coverlet on the divan; the carpet might be thick and coarse, or finely textured and relatively fragile, according to the climate or the wealth of the individual. It is not surprising that the Greek and Latin texts which frequently mention carpets and covers seen by travellers in the lands east of Byzantium (or acquired thence by military loot or by way of merchandise) usually remain ambiguous about the exact nature of the fabric to which they refer. The Latin word *tapetum* could refer equally to a cover, a curtain or a hanging. It is only rarely that one can be relatively certain that it is indeed a pile carpet which is being described.

There are three main types of carpet knotting, the Persian (Senneh), the Turkish (Ghiordes), and the single-warp knot of Spain. In addition, there are loop pile fabrics with the pile run in as a continuous weft which, when the loops are cut, are extremely difficult to tell apart from a true knotted pile. A looped pile is found on Egyptian Coptic cloths of the late Roman period as well as at Dura-Europos (third century A.D.) and at Fostat (the mediaeval site of Cairo). Fragments of pile carpet, some of which were certainly made with a true knotted pile, though others may be looped pile fabrics, have been found by Kozlov at Noin-Ula and by Sir Aurel Stein at Turfan and at other sites in Central Asia; these can be dated between the second and sixth centuries A.D. Fine knotted carpet fragments were also found at Dura-Europos (second and third centuries A.D.). A complete small rug from a burial site in Egypt of the fifth and sixth century A.D. is in the Metropolitan Museum, New York; it has a cut

II Anatolian. Ladik Prayer-Carpet. 3 ft. 9 ins. × 5 ft. 8 ins. Characteristic features are the triple gables of the prayer-niche, the reversed tulips below on stiff stems with jutting leaves, and the pale blue above the niche. The borders are especially colourful and richly decorated, the guard-stripes with scroll patterns.

looped pile. A large number of both sorts have been found in the burial heaps of old Cairo (Fostat) which date from the tenth to the fifteenth centuries, and the single-warp knot has also been found there. The Senneh loop pile was used as a decorative addition to Egyptian linen fabrics of the eighteenth Dynasty, which puts the practice of this technique back to the early part of the second millennium B.C. It seems, therefore, that the origin of pile fabrics is very ancient, and whilst an exact study requires the careful differentiation of loop-pile from knotted-pile techniques, it can be said that pile fabrics, and hence carpet knotting, sprang from a weaving tradition which can be traced back almost to prehistoric times.

The earliest pile carpet which has yet been found is the Pazyryk carpet. In 1924–5 the Russian archaeologist Rudenko discovered some Scythian burial sites in Central Mongolia at Pazyryk in the Gomy Alti about fifty miles from the Outer Mongolian border. Rudenko excavated these in 1947–9 and in the fifth tomb, which he maintains can be dated to about the year 500 B.C., he discovered a Scythian chief buried with his horses and chariot. All the gear was extremely well preserved in hard ice, and part of the trappings consisted of a carpet about 6 feet by 6 feet 6 inches which had been used as a saddle cloth. This carpet has a central field with a quatrefoil pattern which is surrounded by two wide borders, the inner one having a frieze of reindeer, the outer (which is wider) a frieze of riders. There are guard stripes between. The quatrefoil pattern in the central field is very similar to carved stone slabs found in the Assyrian palaces of Nineveh dating from the seventh to the eighth century B.C.; these have long been tentatively identified by archaeologists as reproductions in stone of carpet patterns. The carpet is very finely knotted, but unfortunately an exact account of the technique, with diagrams, has not been published by a textile expert, and authorities differ on whether a true knotting technique or a loop pile was used, though it was probably the former. The pile count is supposed to be well over 200 knots to the square inch. While it is possible that this carpet was of Babylonian or Persian manufacture, it is reasonable to assume that it was of more provincial origin, reflecting rather distantly the metropolitan style of the day. This is suggested by the style of the frieze borders. The Pazyryk carpet undoubtedly confirms the evidence of early Greek writers who frequently refer to the sumptuous carpets of Babylon and Persia, and justifies the correctness of interpreting their references as applying to true pile carpets. For instance, Arrian described the tomb of Cyrus as being covered with tapestry fabrics under which there was a pile carpet, and Xenophon wrote about thick yielding carpets on the floor, which must clearly refer to a pile.

It therefore seems that pile carpets were as much a feature of Asiatic lands in the ancient world as they certainly were in these lands during the period equivalent to our early Christian era. There are frequent references to them in Byzantine chronicles and in accounts of Sassanian Persia. The Emperor Heraclitus is said to have captured from the Sassanians in 628 A.D. not only richly embroidered and woven fabrics, but also 'fleecy' carpets. Theophanes said that these carpets were even being woven in Greece in his day, although they were called by an Iranian name.

The stories which surround the fall of the Sassanian Dynasty harp much on the luxury of the Persian Court, which was overthrown by the sternly simple and iconoclastic apostles of Islam in the seventh century. The fabulous wealth of the embroideries, coverlets and carpets is frequently mentioned. Most famous of all is the account of the 'Winter carpet', also known as the 'Spring of Chosroes', a carpet in the great audience hall of the palace at Ctesiphon. It was described as being richly worked with pearls and precious stones. This carpet was enormous, since the width of the Hall alone was eighty-four feet. It has been doubted whether the carpet could indeed have been woven with a pile, but Professor Upham Pope considers this might not have been impossible, since pile fabrics for saddle cloths embroidered with pearls and precious stones were used by the Shah in the nineteenth century. The throne pavilion of Kosrhoes II was provided with a different carpet for each day of the month, and every three months the repertory was changed, according to the four seasons of the year. Even the imagery of the Prophet Mahomet himself was coloured by the sumptuary use of Persian carpets, for in his description of the bliss of Paradise (Sūra 15) he writes 'They would delight themselves lying on beautiful cushions and carpets'.

From Eastern Asia there is also evidence of the importation of carpets. The Chinese Sui Annals (590–617) speak of the importation of woollen rugs from Persia. But it must be remembered that here again one is confronted with the difficulty of language, since many of the carpets used until Manchu times in China were patterned felts, and the carpets preserved in the Shosoin at Nara in Japan (sealed up in the mid-seventh century) are of this type.

West Europe's intercourse with Asiatic lands was virtually cut off from

Plate 1. *Anatolian: Gilim*
5 ft. 1 in. × 12 ft. 10 in.
Rust-red ground filled with three
hexagons composed of eight concentric bands freely strewn with
ornamental motifs. Grey borders
with geometric designs. The rug is
woven in two parts and seamed
down the middle.

Plate 2. *Caucasian : Gilim*
4 ft. 10 in. × 9 ft. 6 in.

The reddish-brown field is divided into three squares, each of which contains a central rectangular compartment. The ground is ornamented with a trellis of rosettes with minute S-forms between. The upper and lower portions have the 'running dog' pattern and differ from the side borders, which are asymmetrical. The outer border on the right side begins as a scroll and continues with a rosette border. It is seamed down the middle.

Plate 3. *Caucasian : Gilim*
6 ft. 3 in. × 8 ft. 6 in.

The field is divided into broad horizontal bands of different colours with narrow scroll-bands between. The hexagons, like the small crosses, have varying light and dark grounds. Coarsely woven gilims of this sort are used as covers.

Plate 4. *Persian: Senneh-Gilim*—4 ft. 1 in. × 6 ft. 1 in.

The dark-brown field is filled with three concentric lozenges. The inner lozenge has dark red floral motifs on a pale blue ground; the middle lozenge is bright red, and the outer one ivory white with blue design. The threefold border is fawn and light red with a design of crosses and flowers.

Plate 5. *Caucasian: Soumak*—9 ft. 6 in. × 12 ft. 6 in.

Soumak-woven without a pile. The blue border which surrounds a copper-red field is ornamented with octagons with serrated edges and latch-hook attachments. The border is further ornamented with small floral motifs. The horizontally elongated octagons of the central field are typical. The 'running-dog' pattern occurs in the outer guard stripe.

Plate 6. *Caucasian: Soumak*—5 ft. 11 in. ×9 ft. 2 in.

The copper-red ground is filled with small design-motifs. The three large octagons which occupy the field are reminiscent of Turkoman 'guls' and are repeated on a small scale in other parts of the field and in the blue border stripe. Stars and swastikas are prominent among the varied design-motifs. The 'running dog' pattern in the outer guard stripe is typical.

Plate 7. *Persian: Hamadan*—3 ft. 1½ in. × 12 ft. 6 in.

The gold-brown ground is of undyed camel hair. The lozenges which fill the inner field are patterned with bright colours. The three stripes of the main border are designed with reciprocal motifs. The outer border has small stylised figures of men, animals, and rosettes. This type of border gives the effect of a dark rug lying on a larger light one.

Plate 8. *Persian: Heriz*—9 ft. 1½ in. × 13 ft. 6 in.

Sealing-wax red ground with large central medallion. Above the medallion there is a cloud band in pale blue; the corners of the field are reserved in ivory white. The borders are red. The geometrical treatment of the scrolling branches, which cover the ground and indeed the whole design, is typical of Heriz carpets in contrast to almost every other type of Persian carpet.

the time of the fall of the Roman Empire until the Crusades began at the end of the eleventh century. If very few pile carpets had reached Europe before the time of the Crusades, it seems that from then on the tide of trade began to turn. That the pile technique was not entirely unknown in Europe even in the early Middle Ages is proved by the wall hangings at Quedlingburg in Westphalia, woven with figured subjects in a true knotted-pile technique; they date from the twelfth century. By the end of the fourteenth century Armenians were keeping a carpet stall in Bruges. About this time Venetian inventories showed that it was not uncommon for a house in Venice to be furnished with as many as ten carpets, although they were used more for benches and cupboards than on the floor. They were also hung from windows on gala occasions, as was the custom recorded more than a century later in the pictures of Carpaccio and others. In the fifteenth century, Venice had a hegemony of trade with Turkey, the Levant and Egypt, and it was from her ships that the merchandise of these lands was handed on to the rest of Europe. By the early sixteenth century the great princes of Europe all had their collections of carpets; the inventories of Charles V, Catherine de Medici, Ferdinand of Austria, Richelieu, Mazarin, and our own Cardinal Wolsey and Henry VIII demonstrate this. Yet of these collections probably nothing remains, apart from the Hapsburg collections still at Vienna, and the Wittelsbach collections of Munich. We have to look to the painters of Italy and Flanders, who have left a record of the carpets used in Western Europe from the end of the fifteenth century which is by no means negligible. A short study in the galleries of any of the big capitals of Europe will make this evident to the student of carpets. The High Renaissance and Mannerist style of painting did not favour the naturalistic treatment of furnishing, but the story is again taken up by the Dutch painters of the seventeenth century.

As was said at the beginning, we can gain a good idea of oriental carpets from the beginning of the sixteenth century onwards, both from the fair number of carpets which have survived and those that are shown in pictures. We can postulate a very old traditional style of design for carpets and rugs which is clearly evident at this date, and which can be traced back to much earlier times. The basic designs consist of a field filled with a diaper pattern of small motifs, or with a pattern made up of polygons or star forms, or with an arabesque or floral pattern treated simply and geometrically. With these fields go several types of ornamental borders, varying in the different periods. A diaper pattern of quatrefoils is found in the

Pazyryk carpet and also in Egyptian rugs of late Roman Empire period. Diaper patterns are also found on the carpets from the mosque of Al Eddin at Konia (now in the Evkaf Museum in Istanbul) which date from the middle of the thirteenth century; they are provided with magnificent borders of ornamental Kufic. Anatolian rugs of the sixteenth and seventeenth centuries show these basic carpet designs, as do the later Caucasian rugs, whilst the Turkomans preserved the polygonal types of design in a very pure form down to the present century.

But although a basic tradition of carpet design was maintained down the centuries, in each age and country the current artistic trends of the day modified and influenced the style. The Cairene carpets of Mamluk Egypt show the unmistakable arabesque Mamluk style, which persisted up to the time of the Turkish conquest of Egypt in 1517. Persian illuminated manuscripts give evidence that a new style of carpet design came into vogue in the fifteenth century; it was related to book-cover designs and favoured patterns with a central medallion and quarter medallions in the four corners. The court illuminators of Safavid Persia in the sixteenth century introduced a new style of carpet design which was closely related to their miniature paintings. But this style, with its detailed human and animal figures set in flowering gardens, was only possible for the costliest weavings of finest texture, and with the general decline of Persian culture in the eighteenth century, following the terrible Afghan invasions, it was virtually abandoned. When in the 1870's the Tabriz merchants revived the carpet industry of Persia, many elements of design were drawn from the old Safavid style, although in a somewhat simplified form. Sinuous floral forms and interlocking scrolling systems of stems and tendrils again became the hall-mark of a Persian carpet.

This carpet revival, which has continued to the present day, and which has had its counterpart in Turkish Anatolia, has been far more orientated to the demands and tastes of Europe and America than was the case in earlier days, although even in the sixteenth, seventeenth and eighteenth centuries there was a considerable export trade to Europe. But until this century at least, oriental carpets succeeded in maintaining their own unmistakable character; how far this will still be possible remains to be seen.

2

THE CONNOISSEUR'S
APPRENTICESHIP

The question is sometimes asked, what are the best means of acquiring the knowledge necessary to distinguish genuine old carpets from modern and relatively valueless ones? How can one become a connoisseur in this field? The answer is that theory must be judiciously combined with practice. Theory consists in the study of books by recognized authorities; practice in seeing and where possible handling a great many examples. One must look at and study as many carpets as possible and endeavour to identify them by means of one's theoretical knowledge. It is necessary to sharpen the eye of discrimination by testing one's ability to identify a particular piece at every opportunity. It is a good plan to begin with collections in Museums. There one can see authentic specimens and learn to acquire a standard. In England there is the Victoria and Albert Museum, which has a study collection available to the public, as well as many carpets of world-wide renown in its Islamic gallery. The Fitzwilliam Museum, Cambridge, and the Burrell Collection, Glasgow, have carpets. There are many famous collections in Europe, particularly in Paris (Louvre and Arts Décoratifs), in Vienna (Museum für Angewandte Kunst, which includes famous pieces from the old Hapsburg collections), Florence, Milan (Poldi Pezzoli), Venice (Museo Correr) and Copenhagen. The great Berlin collections, unfortunately, were scattered during the war and are not fully rehabilitated, but there are important carpets at Munich (Residenz) and Hamburg.

It is also important to see carpets in high-class auction rooms and on the premises of the best carpet dealers. There it is possible to handle and examine carpets in detail. However, it is advisable for the beginner to beware of bidding at auctions unless he has obtained an expert opinion and valuation beforehand. In the sale-room everything happens quickly and it is easy to be led into a rash decision. On the other hand, it is especially at auctions that one may pick up a bargain. The author remembers such an acquisition at the Dorotheum (the well-known Viennese auction rooms) where he had gone to advise a friend on some purchases. A plain and insignificant rug was being auctioned, which appeared to attract little attention. The friend also showed little interest in it, but was urged to bid, and it was knocked down to him at a low price. After thorough cleaning, the carpet could be recognized as a good quality Kirman whose value far exceeded that of the Indian copy for which it had been mistaken in the auction room.

Some of the best books on the history of carpets contain excellent colour as well as black and white reproductions, which should be known to the student. A short bibliography of useful books is given on page 67.

3

TECHNIQUE OF MANUFACTURE

One should begin by distinguishing between carpets with knotted pile and tapestry-woven carpets, which are without pile, called Gilims. We shall describe briefly the basic method by which each of these two types of carpet is woven. The knotted pile carpet is woven on a loom which may be either vertical or horizontal. The nomads of Fars in South Persia, for instance, use horizontal looms. A loom is basically a frame on which to stretch the warp threads and in primitive conditions it may be little more than four somewhat irregular branches bound together with twine; it can, however, be a much more developed and accurately made instrument with rollers for the warp and fabric. On the size of the loom depends the size of the carpet to be made. The warp is tightly stretched between the upper and lower struts or crossbeams; the warp consists of threads lying close together and run-

Turkish Knot
(Ghiordes)

Persian Knot
(Senneh)

ning the length of the loom. On to these warp threads the pile is knotted. From balls of wool which lie ready to hand, the weaver breaks off a thread of about two inches long and binds this around two contiguous warp threads from the back, pulling it tight in such a manner that the two ends form a sort of tassel hanging in front. No actual knotting takes place, only a looping and a pulling tight. In this way knot (or loop) is added to knot, the word loop being in a sense more accurate than knot, although the final tightness of the fabric gives the loop the strength of a knot.

When one row of knots has been completed across the width of the carpet, a weft thread is inserted in the warp from side to side (selvage to selvage) so that it lies over the odd threads and under the even; the next weft must lie over the even and under the odd warp threads. But to do this no toilsome threading is necessary, for the wriggling through of the weft is accomplished by means of a clever arrangement whereby the alternate warp threads can be raised as a body, thus dividing the warp and forming a 'shed' or opening through it. The weft thread is shot through this shed; as soon as it has reached the opposite selvage it is either returned at once through the next shed (which raises the warp threads which the first shed left down) or this second shot of weft may wait until after the second row of knots. In this manner the weft flies back and forth throughout the work. After each row the weft is beaten down against the knots as firmly as possible to give the knots and the fabric strength and firmness. The process is repeated row after row until the pile of the carpet is completed.

Now follows the last part of the operation, namely, the shearing of the pile, which has to be trimmed to the desired length, for a thick mass of woollen threads is still hanging on the front. By this means, the thick firm pile of a carpet is achieved. Now the tighter and closer a pile is knotted, the shorter it can be cut. A proverb says: 'The thinner the carpet the richer the Persian.' But this does not mean that good carpets must invariably be thin. There are excellent carpets which are knotted so tightly and woven with such a firm weft that they are almost as hard as boards and can scarcely be folded. Tight and close knotting has the advantage that the outline of the design shows clearly and is not hazy; it has the precision of a painting, but loose and coarse knotting gives very indistinct and vague contours. The fineness of the thread used for the knotting is also important, for the thinner the thread, the finer the knotting which is possible. Furthermore, the knotting must be even and regular for the design to show

III Anatolian. Ghiordes Prayer-Carpet. 4 ft. 5 ins.×6 ft. 1 in. The prayer-niche, supported on pillars, is defined by three narrow zig-zag lines and the space above and surrounding it is filled with scrolling, arabesque forms. Above this there is an ornamental rectangular strip, which is touched by the forehead during prayer. The middle band of the border has a Herati pattern; the inner guard-stripe is filled with carnations.

sharply and clearly. Careful and even knotting is therefore a main condition for a good carpet. If one looks at the reverse of a well-knotted carpet the designs and colours stand out clearly. The more exact and sharply defined this pattern appears the better (generally speaking) the carpet has been worked. But in machine-woven carpets such an image appears only very hazily, and this is a useful sign that it is not hand-knotted.

In mountainous regions, where the climate is harsh and cold, long piled shaggy carpets are made. Also for practical purposes it can be assumed that such carpets were made earlier than fine thin ones made rather for luxury. Thick shaggy animal skins must have served the first makers of rugs as an example.

The number of knots to the square inch gives a good indication of the fineness of texture of a carpet, and of its durability. Loose and coarsely woven carpets are less valuable than those of finer texture. One can gauge something of the quality of the knotting by feeling the back of a carpet with the fingertips. The finest textured woollen pile carpets have up to 300–400 knots to the square inch. The Vienna 'Hunting Carpet', however, which has a silk pile, contains about 790 knots to the square inch. To count the number of knots in a carpet one takes the reverse side and lays a ruler first weft-wise then warp-wise, and counts the number of knots to an inch in each case; by multiplying these the number to the square inch is given. This is quite easy to do with a little practice, but one must first make sure that one can recognize a knot unit seen from the back; since this depends on how closely packed is the warp, one must study the individual carpet before making a count. The production of such closely knotted work is relatively slow, but it is a craft traditional to the Orient; it is learned from childhood and the fingers work with lightning speed.

The fringes which ornament the end of a carpet have still to be mentioned. The fringe is made from the loose ends of the warp threads, which are knotted together to make a tidy finish and prevent unravelling, and can be worked in a number of ornamental ways. If the fringe is original (and not applied to the carpet later as a restoration) it must of course be the same colour as the warp, which may be of undyed and greyish wool, white cotton, or in the case of Melas rugs, a dyed colour. Machine-made carpets always have an applied fringe. As well as a fringe, which has often been worn away on an old carpet, there is the web-end or plain piece of

23

weaving which begins and terminates a pile carpet at either end. The edges or selvages of a carpet along its sides are made in such a manner as to protect the weft threads; these are usually doubled or sewn over with extra thick thread along one or more of the outside warp threads, thus making a strong edge.

The weaving of a carpet is usually done by more than one person, sitting side by side. The number of workers depends on the width of the carpet. Much of the work is done by women and children whose hands are small and suitable for this delicate task. The weavers sit in front of the loom on seats which can be adjusted to the greater height necessary as the fabric of the carpet is made (on a vertical loom) from the bottom upwards. A pattern is followed to obtain the required design, usually at the command of a foreman who gives (or sings out) his directions such as 'twice red', 'four times blue', etc. Many carpets have old family patterns which are passed on from generation to generation, and some are so traditional that the weavers can work them from memory. As for the formation of the knot which forms the pile, there are various ways of winding the thread round the warp to obtain a knot. There is the Turkish or Ghiordes knot, which is perhaps the most used, and there is the Persian or Senneh knot. These two methods of knotting differ in the following way: in the Turkish knot the two ends of the thread are twisted each round a warp thread, whereas in the Persian knot only one end circles a warp thread completely. This means that the Persian knot is slightly less bulky, and therefore the more finely knotted piles usually have the Persian knot. It is not possible to tell where a carpet comes from on the strength of the knot used because both types of knot are used all over the Orient and people of Turkish origin have in many cases become mixed with those of Persian stock. It may here be mentioned that the modern town Ghiordes was known to the ancient world under the name of Gordian; and it was here, tradition relates, that Alexander the Great was shown the Gordian Knot which was kept in this city, defying any hero to unravel it. Alexander the Great solved the problem by the somewhat ruthless method of cutting the knot in two with his sword.

As previously said, there are two kinds of oriental carpets; those with a pile and those which are smooth-faced and woven as a tapestry. Both these should be contrasted with the machine-woven carpets of modern Europe, which are mechanically woven on power looms. The smooth-faced tapestry-woven oriental carpets are known as Gilims. Where woven

Technique of Manufacture

with a pattern, the different coloured weft threads are taken across the warp and back for just the area which the pattern requires, as in the manner of Western tapestry weaving. Where two sections of different colours meet in the pattern a slit is formed in the fabric. When the gap or slit in the fabric is too long it is sewn together afterwards. These small slits in the fabric are characteristic of Gilims. There are also Gilims woven as a plain cloth with a pattern embroidered on the fabric. Gilims are often long and narrow, sometimes made up of two narrow strips in the width. Gilims, especially Caucasian ones, owing to their size and shape, make excellent covers for tables or chests. Gilims are made in the Caucasus and Anatolia and also in some parts of Persia. The finely-woven Persian ones are usually called Senneh Gilims. R. v. Oettingen has described the Kurds who inhabit this region as the most accomplished carpet weavers in existence. Small-sized Gilims are known as Kis-Gilims, 'kis' being the word for a girl or bride. Originally these Kis-Gilims, were made by young girls as part of their trousseaux. It is said there was an old tradition whereby they plaited a lock of their hair into the border of the rug. In this connection, it is worth referring to the custom in the Orient of always introducing some feature into an artifact which will prevent perfect symmetry, as a protection against the evil eye.

Anatolian Gilims are usually called after the town of Karaman. Sileh and Verneh Gilims are two well-known types from the Armenian and Eastern Caucasian locality. They are usually left shaggy on the back since the loose threads have not been cut away. A typical design used for Sileh Gilims is a large 'S' pattern. Both types are also found with embroidered designs. Attractive as Gilims can be as floor coverings they will not stand up to rough wear in the way that pile carpets will, but they are suitable for rooms where they are laid on top of other carpeting.

Soumak carpets are smooth-faced like Gilims but they are woven differently. The weft threads are taken over four warp threads and back under two; then over four again, and so on. In this way the fabric is woven, different coloured weft threads being used as the pattern may require. It should be noted, however, that alternate rows of wefts may encircle the same warp threads or be reversed (as is usual) to give a herringbone effect to the texture. Unlike most Gilims the reverse side of the Soumak is left shaggy with the loose ends of the weft threads which have been used. They constitute a stronger fabric than Gilims and their production is exclusive to the Caucasus and particularly to the Shirvan region on

25

the south-east side of the Caucasus. Their patterns show the particularly strong angular character of Caucasian pile carpets.

A full account of the technique of oriental carpets may be found in C. E. C. Tattersall, *The Carpets of Persia*, and *Notes on Carpet Knotting and Weaving* (Victoria & Albert Museum).

4

MATERIALS

Wool is the chief material used in carpets, besides cotton and silk. The wool is mainly sheep's wool, but camel wool is also used and occasionally, for very fine carpets, goat's hair. Camel wool is always found undyed since it is naturally a strong golden-buff colour which, while beautiful in itself, will not take a dye well. Used in its natural state, a well-knotted camel wool rug with light golden brown as its basic colour can look like a sheet of gold in a favourable light; against this the coloured design may appear like contrasting enamels. Such pieces are found among the Persian Hamadan carpets which use camel hair as a favourite ground and border colour. There is also another group of north-west Persian carpets from the region of Azerbaijan which is characterized by its basic ground colour of natural wool.

With regard to sheep's wool, the most important material for carpets, it is the quality of the wool which is one of the most important considerations in a carpet; this quality depends on several conditions. An important part is played by the climate in which the sheep have been raised. The finest wool comes from the flocks reared at high altitudes in the Caucasian mountains and in mountainous parts of Persia and Turkestan. Sheep from low-lying lands yield a coarser and less good quality of wool. Grazing is also important and, it is believed, the chemical composition of the water. Equally important is the part of the sheep from which the wool is taken.

Materials

The finest quality of wool comes from the animal's shoulder, that from the legs and belly being somewhat inferior. Sheep's wool of the finest quality can appear as glossy as silk, and even be mistaken for it. Angora goat's wool excels in its fineness and is wonderfully glossy, but it breaks easily. Where wool is of poorer quality it tends to look dry and lustreless in a carpet. Wool which has come from the carcase of a dead animal is definitely inferior, and its durability is greatly impaired.

Cotton is much used for the warp and weft of carpets made in certain areas. Persia, a country which grows a great deal of cotton, tends to use cotton for the foundation of most of its carpets. In Anatolia and the Caucasus cotton is hardly found at all, the warp and weft like the pile being made of wool. The same is true of the nomad Turkoman tribes of Central Asia. Gilims and Soumaks are always made of wool throughout.

A simple test for distinguishing between wool and cotton is burning. If the end of a thread is pulled from a carpet and held against a lighted match one can tell from the way it burns whether it is made from an animal fibre such as wool, or a vegetable fibre such as cotton. Wool when it burns curls up and leaves a residue, due to its fatty substance, whereas cotton burns to a white ash without losing its shape. This simple experiment will show how to distinguish the difference between the two. The fat content of wool is always present in a carpet made under oriental conditions and even normal washing of the carpet will not completely remove it. After handling a number of woollen rugs for some time, one can often detect the greasiness on one's hands. This fat content is undoubtedly appreciated by dogs, who not only like to lick woollen rugs, but for this reason enjoy chewing them.

Silk, being an expensive fibre, is much less frequently found in carpets, but high quality carpets of court manufacture are occasionally woven with silk warps and also wefts. Its fineness and strength make it an excellent material for high-grade carpets, and silk pile carpets have a special lustre of their own, the best of them being of superb quality; but many third-rate silk carpets have been made for both the contemporary oriental and European markets. Particularly famous are the silk carpets made under Shah Abbas I (1589–1628) and the celebrated sixteenth century 'Hunting Carpet' from the Hapsburg collections in Vienna.

IV Central Asian. Beluchistan Prayer-Carpet. 3 ft. 2 ins. × 3 ft. 10 ins. The ground of brown undyed camel-wool is characteristic, as are the rectangular prayer-niche and the use of boldly contrasting white in lines between the border-stripes and on the trunk of the Tree of Life, which with its leaves fills the main field. Note the subsidiary trees on either side of the mihrab. The top lacks a main border-band, whilst the upper fringe is knotted in contrast to the lower one.

5

PRODUCTION

The production of carpets in the Orient can be divided into three different systems. There are the carpets and rugs made in and for the home; those made in the home but for sale in the market place; and those produced in larger or smaller workshops for a merchant manufacturer. The demand for carpets in the lands of the Near East has always been very great, and carpets there play a far more important role in the household than they do in western lands, where chairs and furniture are so much more used. The nomad tribes of Persia and Central Asia use rugs exclusively in their tents, not only for sitting on, but also to decorate the walls, and as receptacles for their belongings, both at home and on the march. Even in settled villages, carpets are the chief article of furniture in the house. Prayer rugs are of particular importance to Mohammedan peoples since the Mohammedan prays several times a day and must have his prayer rug with him, whether at home or abroad on a journey. Moreover, it is customary to remove the shoes before entering the house; greater importance is therefore attached to a floor covering on which one sits, and as can be appreciated, carpet weaving has for this reason a great tradition of careful craftsmanship behind it. This tradition has been handed down for countless generations, and many families possess their own designs.

A little after the middle of the nineteenth century the manufacture of carpets in Turkey and Persia for export to Europe and America was greatly developed. This was not an entirely new departure, since this trade had existed to some extent in the sixteenth, seventeenth and eighteenth centuries, but it meant that certain new tendencies were introduced, not always advantageous to the carpets so manufactured.

The workshop, weaving to the orders of a merchant manufacturer largely for export, had its counterpart in the sixteenth and seventeenth centuries in workshops attached to the palaces or large country homes of the Shah and the leading nobility. These workshops produced carpets principally for use in these wealthy households, but the surplus was probably put on sale in the market. The finest carpets are those we know as court carpets, some of which were destined to be given as presents to foreign rulers.

It should be stressed that in the modern workshops in Turkey and Persia the carpets are woven and knotted by hand and not by machinery, and that these carpets are basically different from machine made ones.

In the great Safavid period of the sixteenth and seventeenth centuries the principal sources of manufacture were Tabriz, Kashan, Ispahan, Kirman, Herat, and possibly Joshagan. In the nineteenth century the Turkish sultans had a famous workshop at Hereke on the eastern coast of the Sea of Marmora, south of Scutari.

Tree of life.

Tree of life in a prayer rug.

Cloud band.

Two examples of Seraband cone patterns.

Seraband pear
or almond design.

Two stylized scroll patterns.

6

PATTERN AND DESIGN

There is much less symbolism in the patterns of oriental carpets than is commonly supposed, but they do contain devices and motifs which have in some cases a great antiquity. However, it must be borne in mind that many of the strange-looking motifs are in fact simplifications of elaborate floral patterns which ultimately derive from the great carpets of the sixteenth century. These elaborate patterns, greatly simplified, and woven on a much coarser scale, give rise to distortion and in some cases misunderstood forms, which are then wrongly identified by Europeans as animals, birds and insects. Among favourite designs which have a great antiquity, one must mention the swastika and the sun-wheel, both of which are found in neolithic art. The tree, or tree of life motif, is sometimes purely ornamental, but it is true that trees are a symbol of the Persian paradise and are also identified in the oriental mind with a garden, which in a dry country stands in contrast to the desert. Certain carpets known as 'garden carpets' are definitely designed with a formal Persian garden as prototype, containing a river and pond as well as trees and plants.

A favourite motif in Persian-designed carpets is the cone pattern. Sera-band carpets have a field with a regular diaper pattern of cones. The origin of this cone pattern is uncertain; sometimes the cones look like stylized cypress trees, at other times, more like a stylized pear. It became well-known in the west in the nineteenth century as the principal pattern,

32

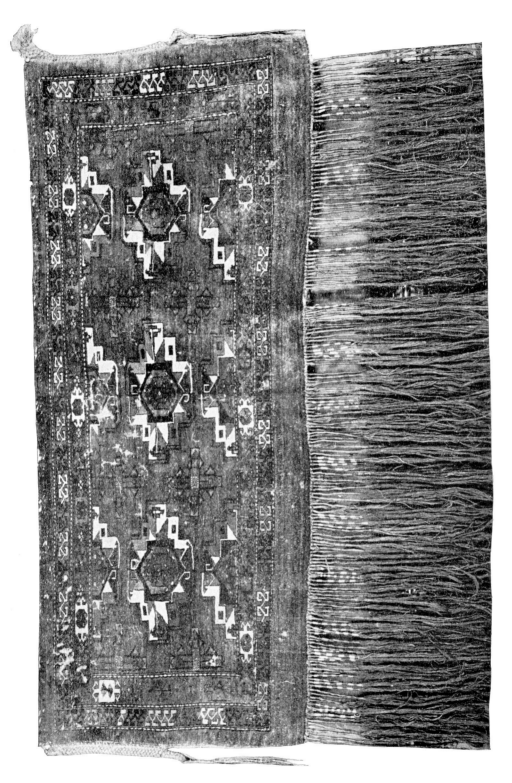

Plate 9. *Turkoman: Yomud*

This camel-bag has a brown or liver-red ground. The typical 'guls' or polygons are striped in red and white. The long tasselled fringe is made from the warp and the bag is furnished with loops.

Plate 10. *Caucasian: Shirvan*—2 ft. 8½ in. × 3 ft. 7 in.

Stylised floral forms and rosettes on dark blue ground; the motif of a camel plays a prominent part. The main border has a Herati pattern in which stylised Kufic letters play the part of lanceolate leaves; the ground colour is black. The outer guard stripe has a gadroon pattern.

Plate 11. *Persian: Shiraz*—3 ft. 10½ in. × 10 ft. 6 in.

The ground is dark blue, varied with much red. The three geometrical motifs are typical, as are the many smaller star and floral motifs which are sprinkled over the field. Animal figures are seldom missing from a Shiraz carpet. The corners are filled with stripes in variegated colours. The borders are richly decorated but the design is geometrical in character. The pile has a particularly rich and silky lustre.

Plate 12. *Anatolian: Bergamo*

The narrow field has a rose-red centre filled with carnations, surrounded by a bold scrolling pattern on silver-grey. The main border has a yellow scroll pattern. The outer border again has carnations on a dark brown ground. The brown inner border is filled with light coloured rosettes.

Plate 13. *Anatolian: Kula*—4 ft. 1 in. ×6 ft.

This type of carpet is sometimes called a 'cemetery carpet'. The dark blue ground of this prayer rug has a pattern of cypresses and willows. The sevenfold borders are in light colours and have a predominating pattern of carnations.

Plate 14. *Caucasian: Daghestan*
3 ft. 11½ in. × 5 ft. 11 in.

This prayer rug has an angular prayer niche, with a floral pattern on a greenish-gold ground giving the effect of flying eagles. In the bottom left hand corner there is an animal motif. The middle border has diagonal stripes in which white, red and blue alternate, which is typical for Daghestans. There are bold inner and outer borders.

Plate 15. *Caucasian: Derbent*
5 ft. 11 in. × 11 ft. 9 in.

The dark blue ground is filled with light blue rosettes and white polygonal compartments connected with an arabesque of leaf and tendril forms. The border is composed of five narrow stripes of variegated colour.

Plate 16. *Caucasian: Kazak*—5 ft. 3 in. × 7 ft. 3 in.

The field has a copper-red ground with dark green in the four corners. The sprawling central motif is surrounded with a white band which is filled with S-motifs. A lilac coloured lozenge fills the central medallion, the main colour of which is dark red. The sevenfold border has a white centre ornamented with a Herati pattern. The design throughout is strictly geometrical.

Pattern and Design

used on a large scale, for Kashmir shawls. The cloud pattern derives from China and has been a favourite motif in Persian carpets since at least the sixteenth century. In later carpets it appears in a very stylized and usually angular form. Dragons and phoenixes are also seen in carpets, usually in rather simplified form. Both these pattern motifs also derive from China. A curious pattern is the so-called badge of Timur (Tamerlane) consisting of three discs or medallions with a wavy line beneath. There seem to be some grounds for connecting this design with the fifteenth-century conqueror of so much of Asia. In central Asian carpets from Khotan the Chinese 'Shou' or longevity character is often met with, as is the meander pattern, which also has its forebear in the Greek key pattern.

Among the best-known pattern arrangements is the so-called Herati pattern, which derives its name from the town of Herati in Eastern Persia (now Afghanistan). It consists of a central rosette, set between four surrounding elongated leaves which curve symmetrically about the centre. This basic pattern repeated all over the ground of a rug is very effective and is met with in countless slightly varied forms. Grote-Hasenbalg has remarked that this design has the peculiarity of looking different from three different distances. From one point, a few gentle waving lines seem to form a pattern; from another, it looks as though divided into neat squares; whereas a third angle of vision makes it appear as a delicate floral pattern without any linear system. This is indeed the charm of the Herati pattern and what makes it so effective for carpets. The Herati pattern is particularly popular among the Feraghan group of carpets. Occasionally the rosettes in the Herati pattern are so drawn that they may be looked upon as representing lion's heads. This pattern is also frequently designed in association with stylized and angular cloud bands which are sometimes regarded as the elements of stylized Kufic writing. Ornamental Kufic writing was a standard pattern for the borders of Anatolian rugs in the sixteenth century and survived among Caucasian rugs throughout the nineteenth century.

Next to the Herati in importance is the Mina Khani pattern. This is made up of a diaper of large flowers or rosettes, with scrolling floral forms in between. Another favourite disposition is the medallion pattern which has a design based on a central medallion in the field, which is surrounded either by a plain ground or by scrolling forms. The medallion is usually repeated in the four corners by quarter medallions. Sometimes the

c 33 H.O.R.

scrolling forms are associated with vases from which the floral tendrils spring.

Floral forms are the basis of most carpet designs, both as full-blooming flowers and rosettes, and as leaves, branches and tendrils. Although these floral forms are frequently highly stylized and simplified, sometimes their natural origins can be clearly recognized. One of the most popular flowers is the carnation, which so frequently fills the borders of Anatolian rugs, shown either in full bloom or as half-open buds. The hyacinth and anemone are also much favoured in Anatolian carpets. So, too, is the tulip standing stiffly on its stalk and with leaves jutting from a central stem, as in Ladik prayer rugs. Indeed, in Anatolia in the spring, hyacinths and anemones flower profusely, and render the erstwhile barren steppe a veritable flowering carpet for a few weeks. From time immemorial the lotus has been a flower with special connotations, and although it can be found as an ornamental motif in both Egyptian and Assyrian art, it appears in Persian carpets with markedly Chinese associations. The peony and rose are also found, the latter particularly in carpets from Shiraz. The palmette is of course a stylization not strictly linked to any particular flower. Among trees, the cypress, willow and poplar can be recognized, and in finely worked carpets one often sees fruit trees.

It can be said that the basic design of the court Safavid carpets of the sixteenth century was a system of scrolling tendril forms. This system has been adopted in many of the later carpets where a much simplified system of interlocking scrolling tendrils can still be recognized, though adumbrated in conception and more angular than sinuous in treatment. When treated in a purely angular spirit, this becomes an arabesque pattern, which is a typically Islamic form of design. It should be borne in mind that the Mohammedan religion, particularly in its Shiite form, forbids the reproduction of living creatures in its religious art; hence originated the elaborate development of pattern systems which, denied the exact copying of nature, sought release in the abstract geometric forms of the arabesque.

It is surprising to find that fruit plays an insignificant role in the ornamentation of oriental carpets. The pineapple and pomegranate are sometimes met with and are difficult to distinguish apart. The pomegranate usually has the connotation of fertility. The vine, so much used in classical art, is never seen.

Animal motifs are frequently seen in Persian carpets, although it is only

'Badge of Timur'
(Tamerlane).

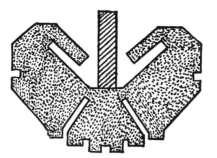

Volute form.

'Shou' long life symbol.

Herati pattern.

Tulip from
Ladik rug.

Lotus flower motif.

Herati pattern (part of).

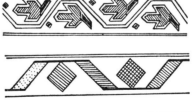

Scroll patterns
from
three rugs:
Shiraz,
Hamadan
and Bergamo.

in the finely-woven ones that they can be at all exactly rendered. In Caucasian and Shiraz rugs the animals are usually shown on a small scale, very angular and stylized. Stags, antelopes, camels, horses and dogs can be recognized and many birds, such as pheasants, turkeys, peacocks, cranes and cocks. The insect-like creatures, tarantulas and scorpions, seen for instance in Turkoman and some Caucasian rugs, are usually the over-simplified remains of some floral motif. Camels sometimes appear in the border of Turkoman rugs and are said to represent a wedding procession. If a small donkey precedes the procession of animals, this is only in keeping with a custom that can still be observed in the orient today.

In the famous Hapsburg hunting carpet at Vienna, which is extremely finely woven in silk, hunting scenes are shown in all their detail. The Persian riders shoot with bows and arrows from horseback at lions, wild boars, stags, ibex and hares which are shown in full flight. In contrast to these scenes, the borders show a peaceful picture of winged genie feeding on the fruits of paradise.

There is a type of Anatolian carpet which is supposed to contain a bird as its principal pattern motif. This is in fact a stylized floral form which has in later times come to take on the appearance of a bird on a branch.

Carpets are occasionally inscribed with a name and sometimes with a date. Texts from the Koran are also met with, such as 'Ya Nabi', i.e., 'O Prophet' and the well-known 'Lā ilāh illa 'illāh.—'There is no God but Allah', which is the cry that sounds from the minaret calling the faithful to prayer at dawn and dusk each day. In Anatolian prayer rugs one often sees a lamp, which is a representation of the lamp which hangs in the Mihrab, towards which the faithful pray in their mosques. It may be regarded as symbolizing the eternal light. Jugs or ewers are often to be seen; sometimes as small-scale motifs they are scattered over the ground of a prayer rug. They remind the faithful during their prayers of the religious duty of cleanliness.

In most cases, the ornamental designs of a carpet are no sure guide to its origin. An exception may be found in the stiff tulips with jutting leaves so characteristic of Ladik prayer rugs from Anatolia. So, too, are the stepped polygons with latch-hook protuberances, which are typical of the Shirvan and Derbent carpets of the Caucasus; but these must be distinguished from the polygons used by the Turkoman tribes of Central

36

V Anatolian. Melas Prayer-Carpet. 4 ft. 7 ins. × 5 ft. 9 ins. The shape of the prayer-niche is a characteristic
feature, together with the smallness of the field relative to the wide borders, particularly the boldly designed
middle band. The predominance of yellow gives a golden appearance to the rug.

Pattern and Design

Asia. Kazak carpets of the North Caucasus, and Genghas from the south-west, are relatively easy to recognize because of the large unpatterned spaces they contain.

A sure sign of Anatolian origin, or at least influence, is one or more inner borders composed of carnations. Associated with Ghiordes are the pillars which frame the niches of their prayer rugs. Baluchistan carpets (from the confines of south-east Persia) have a colouring all their own, and the use of white in violent contrast to the predominantly dark colouring is very characteristic.

But many motifs can no longer be associated with any one place of origin. Such for instance is the cloud-band motif originally taken from Chinese art and found alike in Anatolia and Persia. The cone pattern and the Herati pattern are also used in many widely separated localities. In this connection, it must be remembered that peoples and tribes have at one time and another been expelled from one region and settled in a far-removed area. In Anatolia there are several colonies of Circassians originally from the Western Caucasus. These Circassians, naturally enough, continue to weave the old patterns in their new homes. Inter-marriage between one tribe and another, or between two different areas, also leads to the introduction of foreign patterns. Finally, in the organized workshops of more modern times, a variety of patterns has been intro-duced which derive from earlier designs, just as in former times Turkish conquests settled Persian and Egyptian weavers in their own country to weave their own designs.

Probably the most distinctive carpets which were still being woven in the late nineteenth century were those made by the Turkoman nomads of Turkestan. These Turkomans, owing to their wild life, resisted foreign influence and preserved their traditional carpet-knotting without altera-tion from much earlier times. The basic difference between carpets of Persian origin and those of the Turkomans may be seen in the fact that the Persians prefer floral designs, whilst the Turkomans, like the Caucasians, show a strong inclination towards angular and geometric patterns, which may be due to their Mongolian derivations. These strongly geometric patterns of the Kazak and Gendja peoples of the Caucasus may similarly be accounted for by the Mongol-Tartar origin of these people. Polygons, stars, crosses and such-like angular devices are found instead of flowers, leaves and scrolling tendrils. In Persia, however, there is a group of car-pets made in the north-west, in the Heriz and Gorevan area, where linear

Leaf motif.

Pineapple.

Pheasant.

Turkey.

Peacock.

Two cock patterns.

Dog.

Camel.

38

S-form.

Dragon and phoenix.

S-form.

Bird-like floral motif.

Three borders: 'running-dog' pattern, meander
or key pattern, and reciprocal triangular motif.

Double-T motif.

Stepped polygon with
latch-hook attachments.

39

forms are found together with floral forms. This is also true of Shiraz in the south where the geometrical style is strongly reminiscent of north-west Persia and the Caucasus.

One special characteristic distinguishes Turkoman rugs from those of Persia: the borders of Persian carpets always have a contrasting colour to that of the ground, whereas the Turkomans like the ground colour to be the same throughout.

7

ORIGINS AND ATTRIBUTIONS

I t is convenient to divide oriental carpets according to the chief
regions in which they are made. These four regions are: Turkish
Anatolia; the Caucasus with Armenia; Persia (modern Iran);
and Central Asia. Under this last heading fall Afghanistan
and Baluchistan, where rugs are made somewhat similar to those of
the Turkoman tribes which until recently inhabited Turkestan. Before
considering the different types of carpets found in these four areas, it may
be well to point out that some carpet types are currently known under
names which are geographically quite misleading. First there are the
so-called Polish carpets, which are really silk carpets made in Persia in
the reign of Shah Abbas I. When these splendid silk carpets, which are
often brocaded with gold and silver, were first studied, they were wrongly
attributed to Polish manufacture since some of them bore the arms of
famous Polish families. In fact it has long since been established that a
Polish merchant placed some orders in Persia for a number of these carpets. Also, other carpets of the same type and quality are known to have
been brought to Europe by Persian embassies and presented to ruling
potentates. For example, there are the silk carpets presented to the Doge
of Venice and for long preserved in the treasury at St. Mark's at Venice
(now in the Correr Museum). These Shah Abbas silk carpets are purely
Persian in style and can be closely linked with the decorative arts fostered
at his sumptuous court. A considerable number of them are now known in

Europe, though practically none have survived in Persia, and not all of them are of the same high standard. They have the disadvantage of being readily subject to wear and are often found in very poor condition. It should also be noted that pile carpets were made in Poland in the seventeenth and eighteenth centuries (besides their better-known silk industry for weaving Polish sashes) which were modelled on Persian originals. The true Polish carpets are somewhat like English copies of oriental originals, and while they have considerable rarity value, their intrinsic merits are perhaps not very high. Secondly, Transylvanian carpets were not made, it should be noted, in the Transylvanian district between Eastern Hungary and Western Roumania, but were found there in very large numbers when an interest in antique carpets first began to be taken by scholars in the second half of the nineteenth century. These carpets were in fact brought back by merchants who plied a trade between Turkey and Eastern Europe and were in the habit of presenting fine carpets to the Protestant churches in Transylvania as thanks offerings for successful journeys and ventures. This took place throughout the sixteenth and seventeenth centuries, resulting in a wonderful collection of carpets being preserved in the churches of Transylvania. All these carpets clearly reflect an Anatolian origin. This group of carpets, which has been published by E. Schmutzler, forms a classic collection of Anatolian carpet types of the sixteenth, seventeenth and eighteenth centuries and the term Transylvanian carpet, although it cannot be taken literally, is a useful description for this group.

Thirdly, in the later carpet books there is often reference to Damascus carpets. These were, in fact, made in Egypt at Cairo and their particular arabesque style strongly reflects the art of the Mamluks of the fifteenth century. When the Ottoman Turks conquered Egypt in 1517, the carpet weavers were removed from Cairo; later carpets of this style were woven in Turkey.

There are other names for carpets which are not geographical and which are sometimes arbitrary, such as Holbein, Court, Garden, etc., some of which have already been mentioned. Holbein carpets were made in Anatolia and the name refers to a pattern which was frequently shown in paintings by the younger Holbein (1497–1543) and contemporary painters. The patterns are somewhat similar to those associated with Ushak and Bergamo, which were certainly the places of manufacture of a large group of carpets during the sixteenth, seventeenth and subsequent centuries, but the Ushak carpets are more curvilinear in design and favour large medallions. Other similar carpets may often be seen in the pictures of such Italian painters as Lorenzo Lotto, whilst in the seventeenth century the Dutch illustrators of interiors showed a range of beautiful carpets most of which can clearly be seen to be Turkish in origin.

Coming now to the geographical origins of names for carpet types, most of these can be traced to the province, town or village of manufacture. Nomad, or semi-nomad tribes, however, form some exception to this, since they wandered over very large areas of country during the year. Carpets woven by nomads are therefore called after the name of the tribe. For instance, in Anatolia or Armenia west of the Upper Euphrates the Kurdish Yuruk roam, and the carpets made by them are known as Yuruk rugs. Even here there is a slight misnomer, because Yuruk is really the Turkish word for nomad. The nomads which wandered in the Gehrous region on the Kurdish borders of Persia have given the name of this region to their rugs, which are known as Gherous carpets. In the Caucasus, the Chichi tribe, a Circassian people of the Daghestan region of the north-eastern Caucasus, have given their name to a well-known type of rug. There are a number of names for carpets which have been given by the trade and are not strictly accurate. They usually refer not to the place of manufacture but to the market or collecting-place where the carpets are sold to merchants, and for export. Smyrna, for instance, is the principal entrepôt where many types of Anatolian carpets are collected for sale. So, too, is Mecca, the birthplace of the Prophet, for carpets from the southern parts of Persia. In Mosul on the Tigris, carpets from Kurdistan and north and central Persia are collected. In Samarkand are collected carpets from Khotan and other cities of Chinese Turkestan, whilst Bokhara is the centre for the nomad Turkoman weavers.

Occasionally a special term for carpet-knotting gives its name to a group of carpets. Such, for instance are the 'Turkbaws'. 'Turkbaw' means knotted in the Turkish manner. This refers to carpets from the large region of Khorassan in north-east Persia; although most of the southern and eastern Persian carpets are knotted with the Persian knot, in these the Turkish or Ghiordes knot is used.

The following table sets out the four main regions where oriental carpets were or are made, with specific types appropriate to each region.

43

Origins and Attributions

I. PERSIA

(a) *North*	(b) *West*	(c) *South*	(d) *East*
Tabriz	Feraghan	Qashqai	Khorassan
Heriz	Saruk	Kirman	Quain
Gorevan	Sultanabad	Kashan	Meshed
Bijar	Muskabad	Shiraz	Herat
	Mahal	Bakhtiari	
	Hamadan	Ispahan	
	Seraband	Joshagan	
	Gherous		
	Kermanshah		
	Senneh		
	Mir		
	Mosul		

II. ANATOLIA

Ghiordes
Kula
Ladik
Bergamo
Mudjur
Panderman
Ushak
Melas
Yuruk

III. CAUCASUS

(a) *North*	(b) *South*
Derbent	Gendja
Daghestan	Shirvan
Kazak	Karabagh
Kuba	Sileh
Lesghian	Talish
Seichur	Verneh
Soumak	

IV. CENTRAL ASIA

(a) *West*	(b) *East*
Khiva	Samarkand
Tashkent	Kashgar
Beshir	Khotan
Bokhara	
Afghanistan	
Baluchistan	

We shall now endeavour to describe some of the better-known types listed in the above table, although these descriptions should only be taken as a very rough guide. It is hoped that the illustrations in this book will further help to elucidate the many different types of oriental carpets.

44

Origins and Attributions

TURKISH ANATOLIA

Smyrna carpets

This is a trade name for carpets which cannot properly be designated under the well-known Anatolian centres of production, but which have been collected at the trading centre of Smyrna. These carpets are usually rather coarse, and imitate Persian designs.

Ladik

The prayer rugs of Ladik are characterized by large tulips in their design, standing on stiff stalks and with their heads usually inverted. Another peculiarity is the way the field is divided into two halves, the larger upper part being reserved for the prayer niche and the lower smaller one being taken up by the tulip pattern. In contrast to other prayer rugs, the niche or mihrab of the Ladik prayer rug is composed of several gables. Finally, a good Ladik rug is distinguished by a bright red ground, or glowing pale blue, and often the presence of the tree of life design on one side of the prayer niche.

Bergamo

This was the classical city of Pergamos, situated in northern Anatolia near the coast of the Aegean Sea. Bergamo carpets favour stiff geometrical patterns. The sides often have narrow strips of plain or Gilim weaving. In this they resemble many of the Turkoman rugs, and this may be a survival of the days when the Ottoman Turks inhabited Turkestan. The polygons which are often found in their patterns may be a similar survival. Neugebauer and Troll have drawn attention to a triangular form in the corners of these rugs. J. Orendi has remarked that one often finds in the field of Bergamo rugs some small fragment of cloth which has been sewn into them, or sometimes a fragment of braid, a button or a shell, which is a peculiarity of Bergamo rugs.

Yuruk

These rugs, made by the nomads of Anatolia, have a special feature; namely a border with a single border-stripe. Most Anatolian and Caucasian rugs, on the contrary, favour multiple borders. Latch-hook ornaments are also very characteristic and often result in Yuruk rugs being confused with those of the Caucasus. Ropers remarks that the way the central field is divided with grounds of markedly different colours, and the way the field is contrasted with the border often gives the impression, when viewed at a little distance, of a small carpet lying on top of a larger one. Since the Yuruk nomads wandered as far as the Sea of Marmora and therefore came into contact with many other carpet-producing places of Anatolia, their designs show the influence of these contacts.

Ghiordes

These can be the finest of prayer-rugs and are often distinguished by free-standing pillars which support the prayer niche or mihrab. However, these pillars are not always free-standing and are often treated as part of the flower scrolls which, like garlands, hang down from the gable. From the niche there often hangs a lamp. Ghiordes prayer rugs are further distinguished by their white borders which are richly decorated with floral scrolls. The border usually consists of three stripes: a broad main stripe and two narrow guard-stripes. Red is a common colour for the prayer-niche, whilst otherwise light colours are favoured. There are factory-produced rugs which closely copy the genuine Ghiordes; they were first made about sixty years ago and appeared under the trade name of Panderman. They have the merit of tight and careful knotting, but they are defective in colouring; though superficially attractive, they are regarded by the connoisseur as counterfeits of Ghiordes rugs. Orendi has called them the most successful of all oriental carpet forgeries, but he admits the quality of their knotting. They are sometimes marketed under the name of Kula-Ghiordes, thus pointing to the close relationship of Ghiordes rugs with the next group, namely those of Kula.

Kula

Named after a town in Western Anatolia, Kula prayer rugs resemble those of Ghiordes with their wide borders and restrained colours. They also tend to have a short and somewhat lustreless pile. The borders usually consist of a number of stripes of about equal width and are decorated with little stars and flowers. The field, somewhat constricted by the borders, is often woven in an attractive blue. Even the best Kulas show a somewhat loose knotting. A well-known type of Kula is the cemetery Kula which is unlike any other prayer rug. This seems to take its name from the rows of cypresses which are depicted in the field and which, owing to their association with cemeteries, are symbols of mourning. The trees could also be thought of as willows, likewise associated with death; a mosque is

VI Anatolian. Bergama. 5 ft. 11 ins. × 7 ft. 3 ins. Almost square in shape, with very narrow borders. The design of large angular leaves and rosette compartments is characteristic, as is the use of pale blue and yellow for the former. The broad angular treatment of the design recalls the Kazak rugs of the Caucasus. Note the ornamental motif which surrounds the field just inside the border, and the ewers scattered over the ground.

sometimes seen in the design. Although it is often said that these carpets were used as coverings for the dead, H. Jacobi will not accept the name of cemetery carpets.

Melas

The town of Melas is situated close to the Aegean seaboard. The distinctive feature of the Melas prayer rug is the mihrab, which has a star or lozenge form, whilst the field is often more restricted in relationship to the borders than it is in Kula prayer rugs. In the case of the Melas carpet which is not a prayer rug, the ground is often divided into longitudinal stripes of varying colours and patterns. In these carpets, the field only has a single stripe as border. Another pattern has a field made up of two rectangles with different coloured grounds and filled with different patterns. This type, however, is surrounded with a wide border.

Mudjur

Mudjur is situated in the centre of Asia Minor. Its rugs are strikingly colourful, the mihrab field usually being red. The pile is long and lustrous.

Ushak

Ushak carpets are still made at Ushak, although the sixteenth and seventeenth centuries are considered the peak period of their perfection. Typical of the old Ushaks is the flower scroll which winds through the whole inner field. Red, blue and yellow are the characteristic colours, the former being a rather hard brick red. The medallion is also typical of Ushak.

THE CAUCASUS

The Caucasian region can be divided into three large areas. In the north-east, along the Caspian Sea, is the Daghestan region, with Derbent its capital. South of this is the Shirvan region with Baku and Soumak (Shemkha) as its principal towns. The trans-Caucasian region includes the steppe of Moughan and district of Talish. It has been estimated by v. Oettingen, basing himself on the statement of Radde, the founder of the Ethnographical Museum in Tiflis, that there are 350 tribes speaking 150 different dialects, in the mountainous Caucasus region. Common to all their carpet designs is the tendency to geometrical forms.

Shirvan

Carpets from Shirvan enjoy the highest reputation among Caucasian rugs. The patterns consist of large and small stars and crosses of various

47

shapes. Angular central medallions, sometimes with stepped sides, are common. Latch-hooks are also a typical feature of these carpets. The pile is usually less long than that of other Caucasian carpets. Carpets from the Shirvan region are also known in the trade under the name of Kabistan.

Daghestan

Stripes crossing the inner field diagonally are a favourite design among Daghestan carpet weavers; sometimes these stripes are also used in the borders.

Lesghian

A strip of land inhabited by the Lesghian tribe produced rugs very similar to those of Daghestan and Derbent. They are known for their light colours and a brilliant blue somewhat like that used in Ladik carpets. This clear blue is said to be due to the particular qualities of the water used in making the dye.

Chichi

North-west of Daghestan on the northern slopes of the Caucasus wandered the Chichi (or Tchetchen) nomads. Their carpets have a narrow inner field, often with a dark blue ground which is framed by a broad border composed of many stripes. These borders are decorated with star forms and small stylized floral patterns. The guard stripes are decorated in a similar way and are very colourful. A peculiarity found only in Chichi carpets is a band which winds along the main border between rows of stars and rosettes and divides it diagonally.

Kazak

Like all Caucasian carpets, Kazak carpets have a geometrical pattern, but they differ in that the pattern is large and bold and allows a greater amount of empty space than in other Caucasian carpets. Kazak carpets are often square, or nearly so, in shape. A well-known type is the 'sunburst' pattern consisting of a large central lozenge with excrescences like rays.

Gendja

Situated between Baku and Tiflis and later called Elisabethpol (now Kirowbad), Gendja rugs made by nomads of the region show similar characteristics to those of Kazak. They are, however, often considered to be even finer and more valuable than good Kazaks. In their geometrical patterns they prefer large medallions or concentric star designs, also rays set with latch-hooks and large stepped polygons arranged concentrically.

48

Plate 17. *Caucasian: Kazak*

The red ground is entirely filled with two 'sunburst' medallions, the predominating colour of which is light red. The leaf motif in the four corners and between the medallions is dark blue.

Plate 18. *Caucasian: Gendja*—3 ft. 8 in. × 4 ft. 10¼ in.

The elongated central medallion is filled with brightly-coloured star forms placed on coloured octagons. This motif is repeated in the corners of the ivory-coloured field. The brightly coloured borders are filled with geometrical motifs.

Plate 19. *Caucasian: Karabagh*
7 ft. 2 in. × 15 ft. 6 in.

A chain of medallions only partly
fills the rich dark blue ground; the
medallions are ornamented with
small motifs in light colours. The
ivory-white five-fold border is also
patterned with small motifs, divided by stripes of brown, red and
dark blue. This carpet may have
been left incomplete before it was
finally woven, judging from the
lighter colour of the lower part of
the field and the irregular knotting
of the lower medallions.

Plate 20. *Persian: Meshed*—9 ft. 3 in. × 12 ft. 10 in.

The light-coloured concentric medallions filled with a rather crowded pattern of floral scrolls are placed on a wine-red ground. The main border has a carefully-drawn floral scroll pattern. There are three inner and outer borders, and guard stripes.

Plate 21. *Persian: Kirman*—4 ft. 10½ in. × 7 ft. 3 in.

The cream-coloured field contains a central oval medallion with salmon-red ground. An arabesque arrangement of floral forms fills the whole of this field. The middle border has a dark green ground ornamented with rosettes, which is surrounded by five lesser borders in light red, light blue and sea-green.

Plate 22. *Persian: Kashan*—4 ft. 3¼ in. × 6 ft. 11 in.

The central lozenge has a blue ground and contains a small golden-yellow medallion. The whole field is richly covered with a floral pattern. The wide main border is red and the lesser borders are rendered in pale colours.

Plate 23. *Persian: Ispahan*—9 ft. 8 in. × 13 ft. 2 in.

An arabesque of floral scrolls, in which cloud-bands and palmettes are prominent, fills the dark red field in a lavish manner. The main border has medallions, scrolls and birds (pheasants) on a green ground with yellow guard stripes.

Plate 24. *Persian: Mahal*—11 ft. × 12 ft. 9 in.

The dark green field is filled with flowering trees alternating with cypresses and willows, knotted in light colours. The brightly coloured Herati-patterned border has a red ground.

Talish

From the Talish region on the western shores of the Caspian Sea come carpets which are recognizable by their blue or red field, which often has the peculiarity of being left plain. The borders which frame this field are usually broader than the field itself. This gives the effect of the field being deeply imbedded in the borders, and concentrates the attention on the brilliant single-coloured field. Large rosettes with star patterns between fill the borders. The guard-stripes are decorated with flowers and small rosettes closely strung together. Because of their narrowness and length, Talish carpets make ideal runners.

Soumak

The special technique of the smooth-faced Soumak rugs has already been described. The design of Soumak rugs is also typical; three or more large polygonal motifs fill the field, whilst the interstices are crowded with floral ornaments. The borders are characterized by a scrolling motif sometimes known as the 'running dog' pattern.

PERSIA

Persian rugs are characterized by their tendency to sinuous and floral forms. The carpet trade was more highly organized in Persia from the mid-nineteenth century onwards than in any other of the four regions we are considering. Just as designers of Persian carpets of the sixteenth century were associated with the artists who drew the miniatures and illuminated the manuscripts of the Court, so the artists of the later Persian carpet revival drew on the traditional designs common to the decorative arts of Persia, which are found in the tiles that decorated their mosques, and in their pottery, wood and leather-work. It is only in north-west Persia that there has always been a tendency to introduce a geometric element into the designs. The Shiraz area is also an exception in this respect.

Kirman

Carpets from Kirman have the highest reputation among the more modern Persian carpets. They generally have a light-coloured ground; they are very finely woven and the designs are always carefully studied and rendered.

Shiraz

This city has given its name to the carpets made in the surrounding province of Fars. The Qashqai are one of the best-known tribes of carpet-weavers in this province. They are semi-nomadic and the wool used by them is particularly fine and lustrous; their designs show a geometric character and small angular figures of animals and birds often appear. Their carpets have wide borders, and a diagonal pattern known as a barber's pole is characteristic; they are pliable and soft to the touch and are rather loosely knotted.

Joshagan

This town has long been famous for its carpets, which are still woven according to a traditional pattern. In the Middle Ages the town was the seat of a court manufacture, but it suffered very severely in an earthquake about a hundred years ago, and the village which stands on its ruins is no longer capable of a large carpet production; but the characteristic Joshagan pattern is still woven in the surrounding district.

Ispahan

A carpet manufacture also once existed in Ispahan. The type of carpet now offered under this name is finely woven, with an all-over pattern of sinuous scrolling stems. Medallion patterns are avoided, but the Herati pattern is much used. The best Ispahan carpets rival those of Kirman.

Feraghan

The plain of Feraghan in western Persia has given its name to a distinctive type of carpet. The Herati pattern is used as much in Feraghan carpets as in those of Herati itself. From the same region come the carpets of Muskabad, Sultanabad, Mahal and Saruk.

Hamadan

The town of Hamadan lies near the western frontier between Iran and Irak. It is the site of the Ekbatana of antiquity, once the capital of Medea and the seat of the government of Cyrus the Elder who founded the Persian Empire circa 550 B.C. Wide camel hair borders are a typical feature of Hamadan carpets. The field is usually designed with medallions set in a row and the secondary ornament is sparse and treated in a somewhat angular manner. The effect of the golden-brown of the camel hair in the border and the enamel-like colours of the field is very striking in the best examples.

Origins and Attributions

Senneh

Senneh lies north-east of Hamadan. It has already been mentioned in connection with the Gilim rugs made there. An alternative name for the Persian knot is also taken from this place. The pile carpets from Senneh are finely woven with a very short pile and a minutely-detailed pattern.

Seraband

The so-called Seraband carpets can also be ascribed to the Feraghan region. The derivation of the word Seraband is very doubtful and it is in fact almost certainly a European misnomer, but the rug which goes under this name is unmistakable. The design used is nearly always the cone pattern; the cones are drawn in rows closely fitted together and evenly filling the whole field. The so-called Mir-Serabands are the finest sort. They are distinguished by the smaller scale of their pattern, which is sometimes so minute as to merit the name 'flea pattern'. The predominant colour of Mirs is usually red. The name may be derived from Mirabad, or it may come from the Persian word for the cone pattern, which is Mir.

Kermanshah

The carpets from Kermanshah, a town on the western frontier of Persia (not to be confused with Kirman) used to be greatly prized, but they are now no longer made. The name has been transferred to carpets made by the Kurds in the neighbourhood of this town, which has become a collecting centre for the trade.

Mosul

Situated on the Tigris, opposite the ruins of ancient Nineveh (capital of the Assyrian Empire which was destroyed by the Babylonians about 600 B.C.), Mosul is another market town for carpets which has given its name to a rather vague type. Carpets brought in by the Kurdistan tribes are marketed there as well as carpets made by Armenians, Turks and Jews. This mixture of origins explains the fact that Mosul carpets are of no very certain type.

Tabriz

Tabriz is the capital of the Province of Azerbaijan and is the chief centre of carpet manufacture in north-western Persia. It was famous for its carpet manufacture in the early days of the Safavid dynasty and after a period of abandonment, the manufacture was revived there in the second half of the nineteenth century. The Tabriz carpets of this revival are very different

51

from those of the earlier period. The knotting is often fine, but synthetic dyes have been used all too frequently. Medallion patterns are a favourite design, but the typical angularity of north-west Persia is not found in these Tabriz carpets of the revival period.

Heriz and Gorevan

These are two villages which have given their names to a group of carpets made in the region due east of Tabriz; the Heriz carpets are reputed to be the finer. The carpets are usually large in size and the knotting is firm. Medallion designs are rarely used; the favourite patterns are loose scrolling forms which are geometrically treated and angular; the colours are found in rather heavy masses. In general, the designs on these carpets differ from most other Persian carpets in being much more loosely put together, giving rather a sprawling appearance. This characteristic, together with angularity, makes the carpets of Heriz and Gorevan easy to identify.

Bijar

A town in Western Persia, makes carpets with a great variety of patterns. They may be distinguished by the weight and hardness of their texture. These carpets are, in fact, almost as stiff as a board to handle and they can be folded only with difficulty. For this reason their importation by countries who levy import duties by weight is prohibitive. As Jacobi has remarked, the only way to fold a Bijar carpet is with the pile outwards; if folded the other way under pressure, the warp and weft may easily be broken.

Khorassan.

The region of Khorassan in the east of Persia has produced a splendid series of good carpets. They are still made in the town of Meshed, which also gives its name to the carpets made in the surrounding area which are collected there. Meshed carpets are usually large, with medallion patterns, and they favour a plain ground. They have the cone or Seraband pattern. A number of inferior carpets are inaccurately sold under this name.

Quain

The carpets of Quain are related to those of Meshed. They usually have a blue ground, but owing to the rather soft wool used in their manufacture they are considered to be less durable than the best Khorassan carpets. Altogether, compared with other parts of Persia the wool used in Eastern

VII Anatolian. Ushak. 4 ft. 7 ins. × 6 ft. 11 ins. The principal colours, red, blue, yellow, are characteristic, as are
the arabesque pattern in the field and the angular scroll pattern of the border. Note the simple running scroll
of the guard-stripe.

Persia tends to be soft. Rather similar carpets are produced in the town of Birjand, a little further south. The carpets from all three towns are somewhat difficult to tell apart.

CENTRAL ASIA

We now come to the last of the four great carpet-producing areas, namely, Central Asia, and to the carpets made by the Turkomans in Turkestan. This is a very large and geographically varied area; included are the steppes and mountainous regions of Turkestan, the Turkoman plain, and the more cultivated lands lying around Bokhara, the present-day Uzbekistan of the Soviet Union. To these must be added the lands where the Afghan and Baluchi nomads wander.

The Turkomans

It should be noted that geographically speaking, Turkestan is bordered on the north by Lake Aral and the Kirkiz steppe, which extends eastwards as far as Lake Baikal; in the west by the Caspian Sea, and in the east by the Syr Dar'ya river and the great mountain block of the Pamirs, the 'roof of the world'; in the south by Afghanistan and the Bokhara region. This vast area of Turkestan is peopled by numerous nomadic tribes which make up a population of about a million people. From the point of view of carpet weaving, the Tekke and the Yomud tribes are the most interesting among the Turkomans. The Yomuds wander between the east coast of the Caspian Sea and the river Oxus (Amu Dar'ya) which flows into Lake Aral in the north. The Tekke tribe is confined to the region around the oasis of Merv, the river Murgat and the southern Amu Dar'ya (Oxus). Both tribes, however, sometimes extend their wandering as far as Afghanistan and Baluchistan.

The Tekke Turkomans use a lighter and more lively red for the ground of their carpets than do the other Turkoman tribes, and this has made their carpets particularly popular. The ground colour of the Yomuds is a darker, more purplish red, somewhat the colour of liver. It is a common error to suppose that Bokhara is the correct name for a type of carpet, and the same error occurs in the case of Afghanistan and Baluchistan. It is in fact the Baluchi and the Afghan tribes who weave the carpets, but these tribes are by no means synonymous with the geographical terms Baluchistan and Afghanistan. The tribes are a scattered people who wander over wide regions which, as in the case of the Yomuds, includes journeys as far as Bokhara in one direction and Afghanistan and Baluchistan in another. Bokhara, the largest town in the central Turkoman area, has given its name to the many different carpets which are collected there, and which have been loosely referred to by dealers under this single term.

The name Bokhara, strictly speaking, should be assigned only to Beshir carpets. These are made by sedentary herdsmen in the Bokhara region. Beshir carpets are unlike other Turkoman carpets in that they show strong Persian influence and a much greater variety of pattern than do the strictly formal Tekke and Yomud rugs. Their varied colours and patterns make them among the most attractive of tribal rugs. The typical Turkoman pattern which will shortly be described is not used by them.

Compared with the carpets made in Hither Asia, Turkoman rugs are very difficult to distinguish one from another. All the designs used by the different tribes are very similar at first sight. Geometric patterns alone are used, the floral designs being severely stylized. The pattern is built up by means of rhomboid forms: four, six, eight-sided, or more. These squares, sexagons, octagons and polygons are called locally 'guls', a word which in Persian and Turkish means rose or flower. Each tribe has its peculiar gul, such as 'the rose of the Salors' or 'the flying eagle of the Tekkes'. These guls are arranged in rows across the field; the spaces between them being filled in with small detached geometric designs. It would be too complicated to attempt to describe here the different Turkoman guls, but it may be said that the Tekkes prefer octagons and polygons, and the Yomuds squares and hexagons. A characteristic of all Turkoman carpets is that the designs for the side borders are different from those for the end borders.

The great regularity of the rows of guls, together with a strict limitation of colour, give to Turkoman rugs a certain monotony which seems to reflect the endless uniformity of the steppes in which these herdsmen live out their life from day to day, and year to year. It seems to be equally true that mountainous peoples such as the Caucasians prefer very large and varied patterns for their designs. It must be remarked that polygonal shapes somewhat similar to those used by the Turkomans appear on some rugs woven in Turkish Anatolia. This is almost certainly a throw-back to the earlier origins of the Ottoman Turks who passed through Turkestan on their way westward.

Afghan carpets usually have larger patterns than those of the Tekkes and Yomuds, and favour dark reds and dark blues. The carpets themselves also are larger, indicating that they were made by people no longer

54

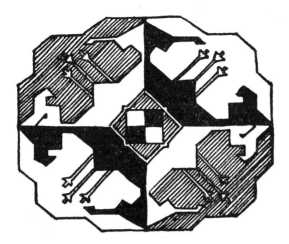

Bokhara gul.

Turkoman gul.

Afghan gul.

55

living a strictly nomadic life. The designs are composed of large octagons which dominate the field. A favourite motif used inside each individual octagon is a triple-leafed floral form. Afghan carpets tend to present a sombre and rather severe impression, but there is a group of gold Afghans in which the guls have a gleaming yellow colour which makes these carpets lively and most attractive.

Nearly all Turkoman rugs have a red ground. It is only by distinguishing its different shades that the various tribes can be differentiated. A very distinctive group is formed by the Baluchi carpets, made by the nomadic tribes who roam within and on the borders of Baluchistan. They favour blues and browns for their ground colours rather than red, the brown being the deep golden colour of camel wool. Guls are absent in their designs. Characteristic is the use of small lines of white which form a sharp contrast with the predominantly dark tones of the carpet. But although this is a distinguishing feature of Baluchistan rugs it is also echoed in those of the Afghans. The contrast, however, is frequently dimmed by discolouration from smoke on rugs which have been used for a long time inside the tents of the nomads. Rugs made by the Salor, Saruk and Ersari should also be mentioned; the two former are much rarer than the rugs already described since in the middle of the nineteenth century the Tekkes conquered these tribes and subjected them, a fate which also to some extent befell the Ersaris.

Samarkand has given its name to the most eastern and northern group of Turkoman carpets. As in the case of Bokhara, Samarkand is really a misnomer, since it is a collecting place for carpets rather than a centre of manufacture. Kashgar and Khotan are the names by which these carpets are more properly known; they show a strong Chinese influence in their designs since they are already within the limits of Chinese Turkestan. The typical design is composed of three medallions spaced out in the field of the carpet, the medallions being rather flattened circles. These are coloured in contrasting tones and surrounded by ornamental motifs such as starlike flowers, trefoil leaves, and pomegranates. The corners of the inner field do not correspond with the central medallion as in other oriental carpets. The borders usually consist of a number of guard stripes. Blue is a favourite colour for the ground and the colours always tend to be soft rather than harsh. The knotting is loose. The distinctive character of Kashgar and Khotan carpets is easily recognizable.

Plate 25. *Persian: Saruk*—7 ft. 3 in. × 7 ft. 6½ in.

A pattern of large floral branches fills a dark blue ground. The middle border has a red ground, with Herati pattern. The inner and outer borders have a reseda green ground, whilst the outer guard stripe has a gadroon motif.

Plate 26. *Persian : Seraband*—3 ft. 7½in. ×6 ft. 1½ in.

This carpet has the typical cone pattern of Seraband carpets; the ground colour is copper-red.
The middle border has a scroll pattern on a light blue ground whilst the narrow inner and
outer borders have the Seraband pattern in miniature.

Plate 27. *Persian: Mir-Seraband*—5 ft. 11 in. × 13 ft. 3 in.

The field has the Seraband cone pattern carried out on a very small scale, which is sometimes
known as the 'flea' pattern. The seven-fold border is remarkable for its careful designing.

Plate 28. *Persian: Tabriz*—9 ft. 3 in. × 13 ft.

The pattern consists of linked compartments formed by symmetrical yellow scrolls, which contain naturalistic flowers standing in a separate vase in each compartment. The rose-coloured border has the Herati pattern arranged in cartouches.

Plate 29. *Persian: Bijar*—11 ft. 6 in. × 18 ft. 5 in.

The centre of the dark blue field is filled with a large light red medallion which is unpatterned. This in its turn contains two more superimposed medallions, one of which is light blue and the other light yellow. The corners have a green ground and these and the inner medallion are ornamented with the Herati pattern. The principal border has the Herati pattern on a red ground, whilst the inner and outer borders have a light blue ground.

Plate 30. *Turkoman: Beshir*
7 ft. 4 in. × 17 ft.

The long rectangular inner field has a purple ground which is closely covered with geometrically-treated floral forms; the three small octagons stand out distinctly on this ground. The wide borders include a main border stripe with a design in yellow.

Plate 31. *Turkoman: Afghan*

The colour of the ground and border is Burgundy red. The large octagons which cover the field are the typical Afghan 'guls'. Each is divided into two dark blue and two ivory sectors; the trefoil leaves are also typical. The side and lower borders have a lattice pattern which is missing from the top border.

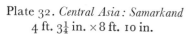

Plate 32. *Central Asia : Samarkand*
4 ft. 3¼ in. × 8 ft. 10 in.

Three large roughly-drawn roundels which are filled with peonies are set on an orange ground. The rest of the field is covered with a floral scroll (issuing from a vase) in which pineapples occur. The corners contain a pattern which derives from a Chinese 'lucky' sign. The white borders are ornamented with a wave pattern which also derives from a Chinese design.

8

COLOURS AND DYES

Perhaps the most appealing attribute of oriental carpets is their wealth of colour, and this depends for its charm on the sheen and texture of the wool from which each individual carpet is made. The splendour of the colours, their lustre and sheen, are perhaps to be attributed to the fact that the oriental craftsmen often come from the most primitive strata of society, living still on a nomadic, or semi-nomadic level, as yet untouched by the influence of more advanced civilization. But they have a natural artistic sensibility, and the simplicity of their lives has led them to develop to a high degree a sense for colour and its complementary rhythms. Their innate artistic feeling enables them to distribute the colours and divide these so that they do not clash, but attain a significant harmony. Be this as it may, the best carpets seem to achieve a wonderful effect of richness and splendour. But it is important to realize the difference between the old colours obtained from natural dyes, whether vegetable or animal, and the modern chemical dyes obtained in the first place from Europe. Aniline and alizarin dyes have been used to some extent in most parts of the Orient since the end of the nineteenth century. These dyes usually fail to impart the glowing effect of the old vegetable dyes, and when bright they look merely garish and crude. The early chemical dyes which were obtained were misunderstood and improperly compounded; most of them proved extremely lacking in colour-fastness. Although the old vegetable dyes often fade to a greater or less extent, they seldom lose anything of their original beauty, and the best of them are relatively fast. Particularly fugitive are mauves, violets and greens. Chemical dyes, particularly in the early period of their use, proved highly detrimental to the quality of oriental carpets. Since then the more far-sighted manufacturers and weavers have avoided this abuse, caused by the importation of cheap chemical dyes, and although an attempt to forbid the importation of synthetic dyes proved abortive, their use has generally become better understood and more limited. Synthetic dyes are found least of all in the Turkoman carpets. In fact, they hardly penetrated at all into the inaccessible regions inhabited by these nomad tribes.

It is always important to establish the colour-fastness of the dyes of a given carpet. This can be gauged to some extent by examining the front of the carpet in contrast to its back and observing the relative degree of fading. By bending back the knotted pile and examining the wool near the knot, one can see how much fading has taken place at the surface. To establish the tenacity of a given dye a rug may be dampened with hydrochloric acid and rubbed hard over the colour in question on the front of the carpet. Most chemical dyes will be revealed by this test. If hydrochloric acid is not at hand a quick test can be made by moistening a handkerchief with water; a fast colour should not be moved by this, but it will be found that with hard rubbing many colours will tend to be moved. When carpets are washed, as all carpets must be in the course of time, dyes which are not truly fast to water will tend to run. This running of colours is always discernible to an experienced eye and is a sign of faulty dyes. It should be remembered that many oriental carpets are made with partly vegetable and partly chemical dyes, and therefore considerable discretion is to be used in assessing their value. The best synthetic dyes will stand up to the washing test, and also carpets where the colours have been fixed with the use of certain chemicals, such as chlorine.

Natural dyes are mostly made from plants in the form of roots, seeds, stalks, rinds of fruit, and suchlike. The colours obtained from vegetable dyes tend to vary a great deal in shade. The reason for this lies in the technique of dyeing into which a number of imponderable factors enter. Madder root is a source for many shades of red, and the age of the root plays an important part in establishing its tone. Blue is obtained from the indigo plant through oxidization with air. From the stamens of saffron, a kind of crocus, an excellent yellow is obtained, but it is a rare and valuable colour and for this reason very seldom used today. Yellow is also obtained from vine leaves and the rind of pomegranates. Dark brown and black are obtained from the gall-nut, a parasite which lives mainly upon oaks; but black dyes usually contain a certain amount of iron oxide and this is a great disadvantage, since with exposure to light the acid tends to eat through the woollen fibre and dissolve it in time. It may frequently be noticed that the black parts of old carpets have worn very much lower than the other parts of the pile. Sometimes this gives the effect of a pattern standing out in relief against a dark ground, but whether this effect should be admired is highly questionable since it is purely fortuitous and it is in fact a defect. In some of the best carpets, wool from black sheep is used; needless to say it does not suffer from this disadvantage. Undyed brown wool from sheep and particularly camels is frequently used, especially in Hamadan carpets and those from the Karabagh region. Untreated white sheep's wool does not look pure white but is greyish or yellowish in tone; if it is not it may be suspected of being chemically treated. Apart from madder, a good red is derived from kermes, which is a beetle gathered from the kermes oaks or cacti. The shells of the beetles are dried and yield an excellent dye. In antiquity, purple was a highly prized colour and was obtained from a certain type of seashell. The legend persists that there was a snail which gave a purple dye, but this is a mistaken idea. Purple is normally obtained from the blending of red and blue dyes. Pink is a relatively rare colour. A peculiar light wine red which is almost pink is a favourite colour in carpets from the Karabagh region. Green is a rare colour for the ground of a carpet since it is the sacred colour of Mohammedans and associated with the Prophet. No believer will step on a green carpet with his feet. None the less, as a complementary colour in the pattern, green is often found in the older carpets, such as the Vienna Hunting carpet. When green is found in prayer carpets, the sacred use of the carpet sanctifies the colour.

Occasionally it will be noticed that a particular colour shows a marked change in different parts of the carpet; sometimes there will be light and dark stripes of the same colour. This need not be regarded as a defect in the carpet. On the contrary it is a sign of a carpet made under simple conditions by a nomad tribe or in a primitive home. The nomad does not want to burden himself and his animals with pots of colour during his trek. He will prefer to make up a little colour, use it, and count on making up a fresh supply when he has moved to new pasture-lands. Often, however, he does not succeed in exactly matching the colour at the next halt where conditions may be somewhat different; the shade of the colour will therefore vary in tone from one end to the other. Often it may be said that these variations serve to enhance the quality of the carpet. It should also be remembered that with Mohammedans a certain unevenness and lack of uniformity in their works of art matches with their religious views, since the Mohammedan does not consider it right for man to create anything perfect. Only Allah is capable of perfection, therefore nearly all Islamic carpets show definite and intentional irregularities in the pattern. One can observe this particularly in the corners. Whilst machine-made European carpets will show complete regularity of pattern, asymmetry is the hall-mark of the genuine oriental carpet. For the same reason the oriental prefers uneven numbers. Another characteristic may be noticed, namely that rugs made by nomadic tribes, and particularly the Turkoman herds-men, are dark in tone, for these people who spend so much of their day in the glaring sunlight find relief and joy in resting their strained eyes on dark colours in the home.

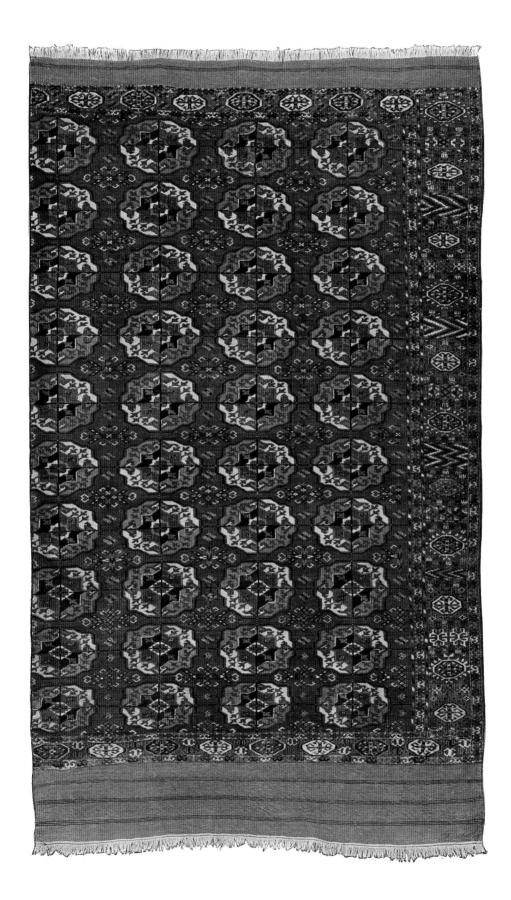

VIII Turkoman. T e k k e . 4 ft. 7 ins. × 6 ft. 7 ins. Polygons (*guls*) quartered in red–dark blue, red–white, constitute the typical field pattern of the Tekke Tribe when these are concentric with a lattice formed by narrow dark blue lines, as here. Both field and borders have a deep red ground, but the side borders differ from those at either end. The octagons (*guls*) in the side-borders are ornamented with latch-hooks. The lower web-end is extra wide.

9

USES OF CARPETS AND RUGS

Oriental carpets were made both for practical purposes and as articles of luxury; that is, for service and for decoration in the home. Among carpets made for use, prayer rugs play an important part. It is quite erroneous to think of prayer rugs as being rare and therefore very valuable. On the contrary a great many are found, particularly Anatolian prayer rugs. Their value depends entirely on their quality, which varies very much in the same degree as do other carpets. The prayer rug is usually of small size, about 3 feet 6 inches to 4 feet 6 inches. The Mohammedan always has his prayer carpet at hand so that he can perform his five daily prayers as prescribed in the Koran, wherever he happens to find himself at the proper hour for prayer; he may frequently be observed praying in public, although at other times he will go to the mosque or pray in his home. The prayer carpet has the hygienic function of preventing the necessity of having to kneel directly in contact with the ground. The rug is spread for prayer so that the mihrab or prayer niche (which takes the place of the prayer niche in the Mosque) points in the direction of the holy city of Mecca. The devotee then kneels on the carpet and inclines his head several times in prayer. Above the prayer niche there is usually an ornamental stripe which is touched by the forehead when the head is bowed, while to right and left of this and a little below it, there is a paired ornament on which the hands may be laid. They may be thought of as symbolizing an angel on the right and on the left. Some prayer rugs have a gable below and above the mihrab and some have a row of gables or niches. Those with five or more mihrabs side by side are for family prayers.

Tapestry-woven carpets or Gilims from the regions of the southern Caucasus, the Silehs and Vernehs, are used locally as coverings for carts

The layout of carpets
in a typical Persian room.

and wagons, and with their gay colouring when seen used in this way they present a very picturesque appearance. Knotted pile rugs are also used as camel and horse bags, also donkey bags. These are laid across the back of the animal and consist of two parts, each one hanging like a large bag on either side of the animal, making a practical substitute for boxes or packing cases. All sorts of luggage is carried in this way, including small children, and it is an amusing sight to see their little heads peeping out of the bags. The reverse sides of the bags are made like Gilims. In the west, the two parts of these saddle bags are usually separated and they are sometimes seen stuffed and used as cushions.

In the Orient one sees cushions of knotted pile fabric used on divans as well as for saddles. They are called Jastik, which in Turkish means cushion. The tent bags of the nomads are among the most beautiful examples of carpet knotting. In the tents, these bags are a substitute for chests and cupboards. The best of them are often made as wedding gifts which the bride works and presents to her husband. They are in their way masterpieces of nomadic art.

As a decoration for their tents, the Turkoman nomads make Kibitka strips which are about 8 inches wide and worked in the finest knotting technique. They are stretched out along the upper sides of the tent like a frieze, and are wound round the tent poles.

The main use for rugs in all districts is of course that of a floor covering. To this should be added that in higher and colder regions rugs with thicker and longer pile are favoured, whilst in the lower and hotter parts shorter piles are preferred. Silk carpets are luxury articles only, and are very often used for hanging.

The normal disposition for carpets on the floor of a Persian room is for there to be a large carpet in the middle; this is called the Mianfarsh or middle carpet, which measures approximately 16 to 20 feet by 6 to 8 feet. At one end, where the host and principal guests recline, is a headpiece, Kellegi, which measures 10 to 12 feet by 5 to 6 feet. On either side of the middle carpet are two side pieces or runners called Kenarahs, along which it is customary to walk. They measure approximately 16 to 20 feet by 3 feet 4 inches.

10

CONSERVATION

A good carpet or rug needs care and attention, according to its age, condition and general state of preservation. Any good rug should always be laid with an underfelt since this greatly minimizes the wear to which it is subject. It is very important to avoid placing heavy furniture on a rare or finely textured piece. It is usually possible to put an exceptional carpet in a part of the room where it is little subject to use.

Apart from wear and tear, carpets are subject to attack from insects and they are also liable to suffer gravely if kept in a damp place. When not in use a carpet should be rolled rather than folded, unless the dimensions render this impossible. It should be stored in a place of relative humidity not exceeding 70°, otherwise it will suffer from mildew and other moulds. This is not only very harmful to the wool, but also affects the dyes, ultimately destroying the colours completely. A good way to store rugs is in an enclosed space, although this does not have to be absolutely air-tight. If stored in a cupboard or chest, paradychlor-benzene crystals should be put in with them; the crystals evaporate and are excellent pre-ventative against moths, which cannot tolerate the fumes. Unless the enclosed space is almost perfectly air-tight the crystals should be renewed every few months as they will be found to be completely vapourized. To render a carpet immune from insect attack it is necessary to spray it with an effective insecticide. A mixture of pyrethrum and D.D.T. is lethal to

64

Plate 33. *Persian: Shiraz*—2 ft. × 2 ft.

This saddlebag has a blue ground with red surround and a white central medallion ornamented with blue lotus flowers between four red leaves. The border has a large angular scrolling pattern.

Plate 34. *Central Asian: Samarkand*
2 ft. 11½ in. × 9 ft. 10 in.

A multiple or family prayer rug. There are seven prayer niches, each with a tree of life worked on a dark red ground.

Plate 35. *Turkoman: Prayer Rug*—3 ft. 9½ in. × 3 ft. 10 in.

The 'Kachli' (cross) design has a ground of deep mahogany colour, but the dusky effect is lightened by much use of white. The pattern motifs are geometric in character; those of the upper and lower borders are reminiscent of fir trees.

Plate 36. *Persian: Shiraz Saddlebag*
4 ft. 8½ in × 2 ft. 2½ in.

The light-coloured design stands out against the blue and red of the ground. Each medallion contains much white and is framed with four dark lanceolate leaf forms.

the grub of moths and most harmful insects to be found in a temperate climate, such as silver-fish and cockroaches. According to experiments made by the Natural History Museum, South Kensington, the best insecticide, however, is lauryl-pentachlorphenol. This can be used as a spray, but it is most thoroughly effective if the carpet is dipped in this in solution with water. The carpet should then be immune for an almost indefinite period from insect attack.

When carpets are in use, it is important that they are cleaned regularly either with a vacuum cleaner or by brushing. It is advisable that only the suction attachment and not the circular revolving brushes should be used. When using a hand-brush, action should always be in the direction of the pile, otherwise the pile is left disarranged and open to penetration by further dust.

Once a carpet has become really dirty, as happens every few years in a modern city, it should be washed. It is necessary to use a good soft water, distilled water being the best of all (but only necessary in exceptional cases). The best medium for cleaning is a mild non-commercial detergent such as Lissapol N, or a first-rate soap. It is after such a wash that a carpet should have a last dip in insecticide to secure absolute immunity from insect attack. It may be noted that this sort of washing should be distinguished from chemical washing to which some carpets have been subjected in order artificially to fade the colours. This is harmful, and a quite different process, and it is to this that the expression 'a washed carpet' in a figurative sense refers.

All good firms of carpet dealers are in touch with repair workers who will both wash a carpet and undertake any necessary repair work. The restoration of knotted pile carpets is a craft which involves the insertion of new warp threads in the worn parts and the knotting of a pile of appropriate wools, which match in thickness and colour. In this work it is very important that relatively fast dyes should be used. This craft is still extensively practised, and although it is expensive, it is possible to save or greatly extend the life of a good carpet in this way. Less costly work by means of darning or patching can also be done on less important pieces. In addition to the repair of worn places in a carpet, it is very important to see that the fringes and web-ends and the selvages are kept in good repair, since once these begin to wear the fabric tends to tear and disintegrate rapidly. Unless the fringe and web-ends of an old carpet are in perfect condition it is customary to have a wide braid or band of material sewn

Conservation

underneath the web-end so as to protect the ends of the woven web when the fringe begins to wear. The selvages also should be overcast with new threads when they begin to show signs of wear, to ensure the protection of the weft threads and selvage warps.

With reasonable care and attention the life of a carpet or rug may be greatly prolonged. Neglected, it can wear out in a relatively short time. If put away and forgotten in a damp storage place or without adequate protection from insects, it may within a year or two be damaged irreparably. The amount of wear which any given carpet will stand depends on its age and texture, and this must always be taken into account if the owner wishes to do his piece justice and to get the best service from it.

BIBLIOGRAPHY

A. Cecil Edwards, *The Persian Carpet*, Gerald Duckworth, London, 1953.

Kurt Erdmann, *Der Orientalische Knupfteppiche*, Ernst Wasmuth, Tubingen, 1955.

Walter A. Hawley, *Oriental Rugs, Antique and Modern*, New York, John Lane & Co. (also London & Toronto), 1913.

A. F. Kendrick and C. E. Tattersall, *Handwoven Carpets, Oriental and European*, Benn Bros. Ltd., London, 1922 (2 vols.).

C. E. C. Tattersall, *The Carpets of Persia*, Luzac & Co., London, 1931.

Friedrich Sarre and Hermann Trenkwald, *Old Oriental Carpets*, translated by A. F. Kendrick, Anton Schroll & Co., Vienna, Karl W. Hiersemann, Leipzig, 1926 (2 vols.).

Wilhelm von Bode and Ernst Kühnel, *Antique Rugs from the Near East*, 4th revised edition translated by C. G. Ellis, Braunschweig, 1958.

Emil Schmutzler, *Altorientalische Teppiche in Siebenbürgen*, Karl W. Hiersemann, Leipzig, 1933.

Amos Bateman Thacher, *Turkoman Rugs*, New York Hajji Baba Club, 1940.

J. K. Mumford, *The Yerkes Collection of Oriental Carpets*, Batsford, London, 1910.

J. H. Mumford, *Oriental Rugs*, London, 1901.

Arthur U. Pope, *Survey of Persian Art*, Vol. III text (inc. carpets), Vol. IV plates (inc. carpets), Oxford University Press, 1938.

Victoria & Albert Museum, *Notes on Carpet Knotting and Weaving*, first published 1920, C. E. C. Tattersall, 4th edition, 2nd impression, 1949, London, H.M. Stationery Office, Cornwall House, Stamford Street, London, S.E.1.

Arthur Urbane Dilley, *Oriental Rugs and Carpets*, A comprehensive study, New York, 1931.

Bibliography

Hamburg: Museum für Kunst und Gewerbe, *Orientalische Teppiche aus vier Jahrhunderten 1950*, Introduction by Kurt Erdmann.

Illustrated London News, 1st January, 1955. R. D. Barnett, F.S.A., and W. Watson, 'The World's Oldest Carpet.'

Natural History Museum (London), Economic Series No. 14: 'Clothes moths and house moths.'

INDEX

Index

Index

Diagonal 'barber's pole', Shiraz, 50

Diagonal division of main border by winding bands, as Chichi feature, 48

Diagonal stripes, as Daghestan feature, 48

Divan covers, 63

Dog motif, 36, 38

Donkey bags, 63; donkey in 'processions', 36

Double-T motif, 39

Dragon motif, 33, 39

Duro-Europos looped-pile cloths, 14; and fine-knotted carpet fragments, 14

Dyes, 57–60; alizarin and aniline, 57–8; mixture of natural and synthetic, 58; natural, 58–9; damp affecting, 64

Egyptian art; see Coptic, Damascus

Ekbatana (Hamadan), 50, and see Hamadan

Elisabethpol (Kirowbad), see Gendja, 48

Embroidered Gilims (Sileh, Verneh), 25

Euphrates, 43

Evkaf Museum, Istanbul, 18

Family patterns, 24

Family prayer rugs, 62

Fars, loom of (S. Persia), 21; Shiraz carpets of, 50

Fat of all-wool rugs, 28

Felts, patterned, 16

Feraghan carpets, 33, 44, 50, 51

Field plain, broad borders, as Talish characteristic, 49

Fir trees, Pl. 35

'Flea pattern' (Seraband), 51, Pl. 27

Floral patterns, basic, 32, 34; bird-like, 36, 39; sinuous, 37, 49; floral scroll as characteristic of old Ushaks, 47; see also Anemone, Hyacinth, Lotus, Peony, Rose, Tulip

Flying eagle of the Tekkes (gul), 54

Fostat (mediaeval site of Cairo), looped-pile cloths of, 14; similar finds at, 15

Fragments of braid, etc., sewn into Bergamo rugs, 45; of hair, see Hair

Fringe: of warp-threads, hand-made rugs, 23; repair of, 65–70; applied, of machine-made rugs, 23; see Pl. 9 for tasselled warp fringe of camel-bag

Fruit of paradise motif, 36

Fruit tree motif, 34; insignificant role of fruits, 34

Fugitive colours, 58

Gables of prayer rugs, 62

Gadroons, Pl. 25

Galls as dye source, 59

'Garden' carpets, 32; as arbitrary name, 42

Gendja rugs, 44, 48, Pl. 18; Gendja peoples, 37

Genghas rugs, 37

Geometrical patterns: Caucasian, 47, 48; Bergamo, 45; Kazak, 48; exclusively, in N.W. Persian carpets, Turkoman carpets, 49, 54; preference for, 37–40

Gherous (Persian) carpets, 43, 44

Ghiordes (town): as Gordian, 24; knotting, Turkish type, 14, 21, 24, 37, 43; rugs, carpets, 44, 46; Ghiordes prayer carpet, Col. Pl. III

Gilims (tapestry-woven carpets, rugs), 21, 24–5; Anatolian, 25, Pls. 1, 2, 3; always of wool, throughout Central Asia, 28; as cart covers, 62–3; embroidered, 25; reason for small slits in fabric of, 25; as strips on Bergamo rugs, 45

Goats' hair, 27, 28

Gomy Alti (Pazyryk), near Outer Mongolia border, 15

Gorevan, 37, 40, 44, 52

Greek key pattern, 33

Green, reason for avoidance of, 59

Grote-Hasenbalg, on Herati pattern, 33

Guls, 54, 55, 56; Afghan, Pl. 31; Turkoman, Pls. 6, 9

Hair plaited into rug, border (Kis-Gilim), 25

Index

Hamadan (Persian) carpets, 27, 44, 50, 59, Pl. 7; scroll pattern in, 35

Handknotting, modern Persian, Turkish, 30

Hapsburg Collection, *see* Vienna

Hare motif, 36

Heraclitus, 16

Herat, 30, 44

Herati pattern, 33, 35, 37, Pls. 10, 24, 25, 28, 29; in Feraghan and Ispahan, 50

Hereke workshop, 30

Heriz (Persian), 37, 40, 44, 52, Pl. 8

'Holbein' as arbitrary designation, 42

Horses in design, 36

'Hunting carpet', Vienna, 23, 28, 36, 59

Hyacinth motif, 34

Ibex motif, 36

Illuminations, 13, 18

Indigo dyes, 58

Inner field with many-striped border as Chichi feature, 48

Insect-like motifs, 36

Insects attacking carpets, 64–5, 66

Inventories of carpets, by early 16th century, 17

Irak, 50

Iran, 50; *see* Persia

Iron oxide of black dyes as cause of deterioration, 59

Irregularities, *see* Asymmetry

Islamic arabesque, 34, 42

Ispahan (Persian), 30, 44, 50, Pl. 23

Jacobi, H., 47; on folding of Bijar carpets, 52

Jastik (cushions of knotted-pile fabric), 63

Jewish weavers of Mosuls, 51

Joshagan carpets, 30, 44, 50

Jugs, ewers, in Anatolian prayer rugs, 36

Kabistan, as trade-name for Shirvan, 48

'Kachli' (cross) design, Turkoman, Pl. 35

Karabagh (Caucasus) carpets, 44, 59, Pl. 19

Karaman Gilims (Anatolia), 25

Kashan (Persian) carpets, 30, 44, Pl. 22

Kashgar (Central Asian), 44, 56

Kashmir shawls, 33

Kazaks of Caucasus, Mongol-Tartar influences on, 37; Kazak carpets (N. Caucasus), 37, 44, 48, Pls. 16, 17

Kellegi (headpiece in Persian room carpet layout), 62, 63

Kenarahs (runners, sidepieces in layout), 62, 63

Kermanshah carpets (Persian), 44, 51

Kermes red dye, 59

Key pattern, 39

Khiva (Central Asian) carpets, 44

Khorassan (East Persian) carpets, 43, 44, 52

Khotan (Central Asian) carpets, 33, 43, 44, 56

Kibitka strips as tent decoration, 63

Kirkiz steppe, 53

Kirman (Persian) carpets, 30, 44, 49, Pl. 21

Kirowbad (Gendja), 48

Kis-Gilims, 25

Knotting, naming carpets from, 43; fineness of, 22–3; loose, of Shiraz carpets, 50; Persian, less bulky generally, 24; numbers of knots to square inch, to count, 23; three main types of, 14, 21–3; single warp, 12

Konia, Al Eddin mosque, 18

Koranic texts in carpets, 36

Kosrhoes II, 16

Kozlov, archaeologist, 14

Kuba (Caucasus) carpets, 44

Kufic writings in patterns, 18, 33, Pl. 35

Kula (Anatolia) carpets, 44, 46, 47, Pl. 13

Kula-Ghiordes as trade-name of Panderman, 46

Kurds as weavers, 25, 51; Kurdistan, 43, 51

Kurdush Yuruk, 43; *see also* Yuruk

Index

Index

Index

Index

Turkoman nomads of Turkestan: late 19th century carpets of, 37, 53; guls of, 55; geometric angular patterns in, 37, 45; carpets generally, 53–4; Bokhara as centre, 43; synthetic dyes least common in, 58; tend to be dark in colour, 60; wool shortage, 28; *for* Turkoman carpets, *see* Pl. 9 (Yomud); Pl. 30 (Beshir); Pl. 31 (Afghan); Pl. 35 ('Kachli' [cross] design) Col. Pl. VIII (Tekke)

Turkoman Kibitza strips as tent decoration, 63

Underfelts, 64

Unpatterned areas in carpets, as Kazak and Genghas characteristic, 37, 48

Uses of rugs and carpets, 61–3

Ushak (Anatolia) carpets, 44, 47, Col. Pl. VII; similarity of 'Holbeins' to, 42, 43

Ushak medallion, 47

Uzbekistan, 53

Vacuum cleaning, 65

Variations in colour-shades explained, 59–60

Vegetable and natural dyes, fading of, 57–8

Venice, St. Mark's, Persian silk carpets formerly in treasury of, 41; in 14th century, 17

Verneh (Eastern Caucasian) carpets, 44, 62; Gilims, 25

Vertical looms, 21, 24

Vienna, Hapsburg collection, 17, 19; 'Hunting carpet', 23, 28, 36; explanation of green in, 59

Vine, absent from Oriental carpet patterns, 34

Vine leaves, as yellow-dye source, 59

Volute form, 35

'Washed' carpet (artificially faded), 65

Washing of carpets, 59, 65

Web-ends, 23–4, 65–6

Wedding-procession in design, 36

White: in Baluchistan carpets, 37; in alternating stripes with blue and red in Daghestan carpets, Pl. 14; on Ghiordes prayer-rug borders, 46; in small lines, on Baluchistans and Afghans, 56

Wild boar motif, 36

Willow tree motif, 34, 46, Pl. 24

Winged genie, 36

'Winter' ('Spring of Chosroes') carpet, 16

Wittelsbach collection, Munich, 17

Wool, as chief carpet material, 27; from black sheep, 59; from Caucasus, 28; soft, of Eastern Persia, 52–3; untreated, 59; *see also* Camel, Goat

Xenophon, 16

'Ya Nabi' text in design, 36

Yellow dyes, sources of, 58, 59

Yomud (Turkoman) carpets, 53, 54, Pl. 9

Yuruk (Anatolia) carpets, 43, 45